THE SPORTS CURMUDGEON

**George Sullivan
and
Barbara Lagowski**

WARNER BOOKS

A Time Warner Company

Warner Books, Inc., 1271 Avenue of the Americas, New York, NY 10020
W A Time Warner Company

Printed in the United States of America

First printing: April 1993

10 9 8 7 6 5 4 3 2 1

Library of Congress Cataloging-in-Publication Data

Sullivan, George
    The sports curmudgeon / George Sullivan and Barbara Lagowski.
        p.   cm.
    ISBN 0-446-39399-1
    1. Sports—Quotations, maxims, etc.   2. Sports—Humor.
I. Lagowski, Barbara J.   II. Title.
GV707.S88   1993
796'.0207—dc20   92-30856
                                                                          CIP

Cover design by Diane Luger
Cover illustration by Victor Vaccaro
Book design by L. McRee

GIVE 'EM THE RASPBERRIES!

Spanning the globe for the wildest sendups and wittiest putdowns in baseball, football, basketball, boxing, hockey, and even bocce ball, *The Sports Curmudgeon* is truly a disgruntled fan's dream. Packed with more fast and furious jabs than a Muhammad Ali fight, here is a forum for the greatest offsides comments and off-color slams ever scored by the legendary curmudgeons of pro sports, including:

"I never took the game home with me. I always left it in some bar."
—*Bob Lemon*

"We're the only team in history that could
lose nine games in a row and then go into a slump."
—*Bill Fitch*

"Boxing is sort of like jazz. The better it is,
the less amount of people can appreciate it."
—*George Forman*

"Statistics are about as interesting as first-base coaches."
—*Steve Sax*

"I want to be the fastest woman in the world—
in a manner of speaking."
—*Shirley "Cha-Cha" Muldowney*

"Pour hot water over a sportswriter
and you get instant horseshit."
—*Ted Williams*

"I never cease to amaze myself. I say this humbly."
—*Don King*

"This fresh and original compilation of wit and wisdom gentle and barbed will evoke smiles and laughter in everyone, curmudgeons included."
—Donald Honig, baseball historian and author of *Baseball America, Baseball: The Illustrated History of America's Game,* and other books.

**This book is for each other.
We deserve it—and each other.**

Sports curmudgeons always have their say, no matter what the obstacle.

So this book is also dedicated to Luther "Dummy" Taylor, a deaf-mute pitcher for the New York Giants at the turn of the century. He once was ejected from a game for cursing an umpire—in sign language.

He's our kind of guy—and what this book is all about.

As we stand here wai-ting
for the ball game to start...

—Comic Albert Brooks'
curmudgeonly improvement
on the first line of "The Star-
Spangled Banner"

Introduction

$5 Million and a No-Trade Clause
Do Not Buy Happiness

Maybe it's because they spend so much time on the road. (As sports journalist Harold Rosenthal once said, the road "will make a bum out of the best of them.")

Or maybe it's because our professional athletes have lost sight of the higher ideals of sport. (Wide receiver Fred Biletnikoff said it best: "Anybody who says they're not in it for the money is full of shit.")

Whatever the reason, sour grapes have replaced Wheaties as the "breakfast of champions"—and this book dishes up a hearty helping.

Curmudgeons—loosely defined as those who have swallowed so many bitter pills that they have actually *become* bitter pills—aren't born but made. And professional sports have helped make curmudgeons out of many of us. As fans, we have been subjected to blowhard executives, crybaby managers, sexually "addicted" players, money-grubbing college athletes, walkouts, lockouts, and even fixes. Our two-dollar bleacher seats have been tarted up and turned into six-figure luxury boxes. Some of us—including the authors of this book, who grew up on opposite ends of Massachusetts—were even turned into Red Sox fans as innocent children. Need we say more?

For the thousands of literate malcontents who scan the papers daily for the kind of quotes that can give even a sport like boxing a black eye, this book will be just what the fight doctor ordered. But for those clinging to the idea that *something* in sports must still be sacred, we offer this parting shot from Hall of Fame pitcher–turned–broadcaster Don Drysdale: "When we played, World Series checks meant something. Now all they do is screw up your taxes."

May this book screw up ours.

—George Sullivan and Barbara Lagowski

THE SPORTS CURMUDGEON

Addresses

Mr. Casey Stengel
Psychiatric Ward
St. Elizabeth's Hospital
Boston, Mass.

> —FRANKIE FRISCH, Pittsburgh Pirates
> manager, addressing get-well wishes to
> crony Casey Stengel, Boston Braves man-
> ager, whose shattered leg was in traction
> after he was struck by an automobile two
> days before the start of the 1943 season

The wire's message wasn't any more sympathetic. It read: "Your attempt at suicide fully understood. Deepest sympathy you didn't succeed."

Western Union had difficulty locating Stengel at that. Casey was bedded down in the maternity ward due to a wartime shortage of hospital beds.

Adultery

That would be like playing the same golf course all the time.

> —SEVERIANO BALLESTEROS, pro golfer,
> on monogamy

Dear, make all the substitutions you want. Just don't carry it over into your personal life.

> —MARY HENSON, wife of Illinois basketball coach
> Lou Henson, who had been criticized for his substitutions

If you don't get it by midnight, chances are you ain't gonna get it, and if you do it ain't worth it.

> —CASEY STENGEL

Where's your wife, pal? One of our players is missing.

> —JIMMY PIERSALL, outfielder, to a taunting bleacher
> fan

We try to lead good clean lives, but whether or not we do is for our wives to decide.

> —BOB DERNIER, outfielder

Obviously, I didn't know my wife was coming tonight or I wouldn't have invited you to dinner.

> —MIKE MARSHALL, pitcher, to a dinner companion, as quoted by his ex-wife Nancy

Advertising

The people in football don't want you to associate their sport in any way with drugs. They want you to associate it with alcohol.

> —DAVE BARRY, columnist

Don't quote me on this, but if they ever manage to ban beer advertising in baseball you can kiss the national pastime goodbye.

> —ROGER MARIS, Baseball Hall of Famer and beer distributor

Agents

When they smile, blood drips off their teeth.

> —TED TURNER, Atlanta Braves owner

I'm not an agent. I'm an engineer of careers.

> —MARK McCORMACK, agent

Why should I give somebody 10 percent when I do all the work?

> —MARK "THE BIRD" FIDRYCH, Detroit Tigers pitcher

When I negotiated Bob Stanley's contract with the Red Sox, we had statistics demonstrating he was the third best pitcher in the league. They had a chart showing he was the sixth best pitcher on the Red Sox.

—BOB WOOLF, agent

A complete ballplayer today is one who can hit, field, run, throw, and pick the right agent.

—BOB LURIE, San Francisco Giants owner

We're doing this whole thing backward. Attorneys should wear numbers on their backs and box scores should have entries for writs, depositions, and appeals.

—BILL VEECK, Baseball Hall of Fame owner and showman

Aging

It's hell to get older.

—BABE RUTH, late in his career

They tell you that things change at 40, but they don't tell you how much.

—JOHNNY UNITAS, Hall of Fame quarterback

When I get to be 40 I'm going to charge people to watch me get out of bed.

—DAVE HERMAN, lineman

In other jobs you get old, big deal. In football you get old, you're fired.

> —DEACON JONES, defensive end

When you get too old to chase other things, you can always chase golf balls.

> —ANONYMOUS

When you're too young to take up golf and too old to rush up on the net.

> —FRANKLIN PIERCE ADAMS, humorist, pinpointing middle age

Old golfers never die. They just lose their balls.

> —ANONYMOUS

When I was 40, my doctor advised me that a man in his forties shouldn't play tennis. I heeded his advice carefully and could hardly wait until I reached 50 to start again.

> —HUGO BLACK, Supreme Court justice

Age is mind over matter. As long as you don't mind, it don't matter.

> —MUHAMMAD ALI

After 35, you're on a pass.

> —TED WILLIAMS

First your legs go. Then you lose your friends.

>   —WILLIE PEP, boxing Hall of Famer

First you forget names. Then you forget faces. Then you forget to zip up your fly. And then you forget to unzip your fly.

>   —BRANCH RICKEY, as an aging baseball executive

I'll never make the mistake of being 70 again.

>   —CASEY STENGEL

You start chasing a ball and your brain immediately commands your body to "Run forward! Bend! Scoop up the ball! Peg it to the infield!" Then your body says, "Who, me?"

>   —JOE DiMAGGIO

He's learning to say hello when it's time to say goodbye.

>   —FRANK GRAHAM, SR., sportswriter, on New York Yankees grump Bob Meusel, who mellowed as retirement approached

Retire? Retire and do what? I already fish and play golf.

>   —JULIUS BOROS, pro golfer, at age 60

The question isn't at what age I want to retire. It's at what income.

>   —GEORGE FOREMAN, heavyweight champion

The older they get the better they were when they were younger.

—JIM BOUTON, pitcher turned author

The Agony of Defeat

The last one.

—BRUCE WOODCOCK, KO'd boxer, when asked
which of Tami Mauriello's punches bothered him most

The All-American Pastime

All the balls are made in Haiti now...and most of the gloves are made in Taiwan.

—ANDY ROONEY, humorist, revealing some of the
qualifications that make baseball our national game

Appearances

There are two styles of nose which all prize fighters must be content to select from, one presenting a flat triangular appearance, the other indented near the top and slightly turned up, so that you could hang a key on it. The immortal Heenan had a moderate nose of the last pattern.

—CHARLES DICKENS, on the 1860 fight between
American John Heenan and Briton Tom Sayers in
the first international white heavyweight title bout

Held in Farnborough, England, the bout ended in a draw after 42 rounds— two hours and twenty minutes—when the crowd sensed the Yank was winning and broke down the ring.

Not like Frank Gifford. Just handsome, like a man.

> —LOU MICHAELS, veteran defensive lineman, describing his father—and also a certain fellow footballer

So I'm ugly. I never saw anyone hit with his face.

> —YOGI BERRA

I've got a face made for radio.

> —RON LUCIANO, umpire turned television commentator

I've found that you don't need a necktie if you can hit.

> —TED WILLIAMS, who preferred hitting to wearing neckties

Astroturf

If horses won't eat it, I don't want to play on it.

> —DICK ALLEN, slugger and philosopher

Athletes

In my younger days it was not considered respectable to be an athlete. An athlete was always a man that was not strong enough to work.

> —FINLEY PETER DUNNE, humorist

An athlete has such a narrow view of life he does not know reality.

> —BRUCE JENNER, Olympic decathlon champion

Autographs

Any ballplayer that don't sign autographs for little kids ain't American. He's a communist.

> —ROGERS HORNSBY, hard-hitting and hard-bitten Baseball Hall of Famer

$45 per signing. No bats.

> —An autograph show sign detailing what it takes to get a Baseball Hall of Famer's autograph in 1991

I seldom refused autograph-seekers, unless they were old enough to look like collection agents.

> —JOE PEPITONE, veteran major leaguer

Oh, hell, who wants to collect that crap?

> —BABE RUTH, on autograph hunting

Auto Racing

Cars are used in this entertainment because the SPCA frowns on using lions.

> —RED SMITH, Pulitzer Prize–winning columnist

It's not so much a sporting event as a deathwatch. They hold it, fittingly, on Memorial Day.

> —JIM MURRAY, another Pulitzer Prize winner, on the Indianapolis 500

It is necessary to relax your muscles when you can. Relaxing your brain is fatal.

> —STIRLING MOSS, British auto racer

On the day of the race, a lot of people want you to sign something just before you get in the car so that they can say they got your last autograph.

> —A. J. FOYT, champion driver

This is a sport?

> —RED SMITH, columnist

Not everyone kills himself with a rope or a gun. Auto drivers at high speed are committing suicide, but how long it takes them is up to them and chance....

> —DR. KARL MENNINGER, American psychiatrist

Gentlemen, go to your tomb.

> —A popular alternative to the ubiquitous "Gentlemen, start your engines"

Gentlemen, start your coffins.

> —JIM MURRAY, columnist, on the Indy 500

Auto Racing, Women's Division

I want to be the fastest woman in the world—in a manner of speaking.

> —SHIRLEY "CHA-CHA" MULDOWNEY, race-car driver

You drive the car, you don't carry it.

> —JANET GUTHRIE, first woman to compete in Indy 500 in 1977, suggesting the relative unimportance of physical strength in driving a race car

Awards

I'm very glad to receive the Klem award, but I'll tell you the truth: Klem hated my guts and I hated his.

> —BEANS REARDON, retired umpire, accepting the award named for umpiring pioneer Bill Klem

Bachelors

Never get married in the morning, 'cause you never know who you'll meet that night.

> —PAUL HORNUNG, Football Hall of Famer

I'm not married, but I'm in great demand.

> —LEROY "SATCHEL" PAIGE, Baseball Hall of Famer

A Backhanded Compliment

Cobb is a prick. But he can hit, God Almighty, that man can hit.

> —BABE RUTH, on lifelong adversary Ty Cobb

Bare Facts

I didn't see that he had anything to be proud of.

> —BUDDY RYAN, NFL coach, commenting
> on a streaker who had raced across the field

Baseball

Baseball is America's favorite sport because it's so slow. Any idiot can follow it. And just about any idiot can play it.

> —GENE VIDAL, quoted by his literary son, Gore
> Vidal, from Gore's book *Matters of Fact and Fiction*

A critic once characterized baseball as six minutes of action crammed into two and one-half hours.

> —RAY FITZGERALD, sportswriter

Baseball is a kid's game that grownups only tend to screw up.

> —BOB LEMON, pitcher, manager, and Hall of Famer

Baseball has always chosen the longest way around and has never been administered with any real intelligence.

> —PAUL GALLICO, writer

The trouble with the big leagues is that there aren't enough big leaguers.

> —JIMMY CANNON, columnist

A baseball game is twice as much fun if you watch it on company time.

> —WILLIAM C. FEATHER

Baseball must be a great game to survive the people who run it.

> —Unknown curmudgeon, quoted by columnist Arthur Daley

No game that can be played by a person with a wad of tobacco in his mouth is a sport.

> —ANDY ROONEY, humorist

Baseball isn't a business. It's more like a disease.

> —WALTER O'MALLEY, businessman and baseball team owner, who moved his Dodgers from Brooklyn to Los Angeles

Baseball and malaria keep coming back.

>　　—GENE MAUCH, manager

In baseball, you don't know *nothing*.

>　　—YOGI BERRA

Baseball Commissioners

Bowie Kuhn is the biggest jerk in the history of baseball.

>　　—CHARLES O. FINLEY, Oakland A's owner

Happy [Chandler] left office for reasons of health; that is, the owners got sick of him.

>　　—RED SMITH, columnist

There was a vacancy when I left, and the owners decided to continue with it.

>　　—A. B. "HAPPY" CHANDLER, baseball commissioner, on successor Ford Frick

The Unknown Soldier.

>　　—Popular reference to William "Spike" Eckert, the retired air force general few baseball executives or fans had heard of before he became commissioner

The owners played two dirty tricks on [Spike Eckert], in 1965 when they hired him and in 1968 when they fired him.

—RED SMITH, columnist

We already have a dead man on the job.

—EDWARD BENNETT WILLIAMS, Baltimore Orioles owner, when someone said the late Walter O'Malley had been proposed as commissioner

[Judge Landis] really knew little about the game. He didn't know a baseball from a bale of hay. . . .

He was hired to look mean, and he played the part. I don't think he liked going to ball games, and didn't go very often. But I've seen some pictures of him and the cameraman always seemed to catch him in the same posture.

Landis' fist would be under his chin, his white hair ruffled and flying, his face creased in an ugly scowl. Precisely what he saw going on out in the field, I can't say. . . . He might have been sitting there, just puzzling.

—A. B. "HAPPY" CHANDLER, baseball commissioner, on his predecessor, Kenesaw Mountain Landis

Other than a tack on his seat, nothing could make [Bowie] Kuhn jump faster than when he saw a television camera.

—RED SMITH, columnist

Baseball Ethics

If they throw one at your head, you throw twice [at their heads]. If they throw twice, you throw four times.

—LEO DUROCHER, advising his pitchers

Baseball Fans

Baseball mainly attracts two demographic groups: boys under 14 and men over 60. Boys under 14 like it because their daddies made them play catch in the yard. Men over 60 like it because they have to piss a lot and they can do this while watching baseball on TV and not miss anything.

—DAN JENKINS, novelist and humorist

Baseball Players, Innate Intelligence of

Tell a ballplayer something a thousand times, then tell him again, because that might be the time he'll understand something.

—PAUL RICHARDS, who knew from a dozen years managing in the major leagues

Baseball vs. Cricket

Baseball has the great advantage over cricket of being sooner ended.

—GEORGE BERNARD SHAW

Baseball vs. Football

In football the object is to march into enemy territory and cross his goal. In baseball the object is to go home.

> —GEORGE CARLIN, comic

Base Stealing

His head was full of larceny, but his feet were honest.

> —ARTHUR "BUGS" BAER, columnist, on slow-footed New York Yankee Ping Bodie's difficulty stealing bases

Basketball

It's a simple game to understand. Players race up and down a fairly small area indoors and stuff the ball into a ring with Madonna's dress hanging on it.

> —DAN JENKINS, novelist and humorist

I consider playing basketball...the most shallow thing in the world.

> —BILL RUSSELL, Basketball Hall of Famer

The only thing in this country that blacks really dominate, except for poverty, is basketball.

> —AL McGUIRE, basketball player, coach, and broadcaster

Basketball Logic

If you give a guy three points for a long shot, then you should give him just one point for a layup.

>   —ARNOLD "RED" AUERBACH, Boston Celtics
>   coaching legend who opposed NBA adoption of
>   the three-point shot

Basketball vs. Football

To play basketball you have to be seven-foot-six. To play football you have to be the same width.

>   —BILL VEECK, Baseball Hall of Fame owner and
>   showman

Beauty

The designated gerbil.

>   —BILL LEE, on his pouch-cheeked Boston Red
>   Sox manager, Don Zimmer

If you slid into bases head first for 20 years, you'd be ugly, too.

>   —PETE ROSE

Bell? Hell!

Please, not here, not now, don't fight for free. This is for big money!

>   —DON KING, boxing promoter, when heavyweights
>   Larry Holmes and Gerry Cooney began mixing it
>   up during a prefight press conference

Biathlon

A Russian puts on a pair of skis, picks up a rifle, slides around in the trees, and stops every so often to shoot a West German.

> —DAN JENKINS, novelist and humorist,
> clarifying the often misunderstood sport
> of biathlon

Billiards

To play billiards well is a sign of a misspent youth.

> —HERBERT SPENCER, English philosopher

Bobsledding

This is a sport in which demented people sit on a sled that goes 2,000 miles per hour down an ice ditch. The same sport is often practiced without ice—when four drunks leave a fraternity party in a BMW.

> —DAN JENKINS, novelist and humorist

Bodybuilding

The thing that's wrong with [bodybuilders] is that they have developed those muscles with no intention of doing anything with them except showing them off.

> —ANDY ROONEY, humorist

Boxing

The manly art of modified murder.

> —W. O. McGEEHAN, columnist, defining boxing

Boxing . . . is a nasty, brutish activity whose point is to attack the very source of civilization, the human brain.

> —CHRISTOPHER LEHMANN-HAUPT, columnist

Boxing is a great sport and a dirty business.

> —KEN NORTON, heavyweight champion

Boxing is sort of like jazz. The better it is, the less amount of people can appreciate it.

> —GEORGE FOREMAN, heavyweight champion

Who would pay a nickel for another Patterson-Liston fight? I know I wouldn't.

> —FLOYD PATTERSON, after being knocked out by Sonny Liston in two heavyweight title bouts—both times in the first round—was never matched with him again

I am boxing.

> —MUHAMMAD ALI

The hardest thing about prize fightin' is pickin' up yer teeth with a boxing glove on.

> —FRANK McKINNEY "KIN" HUBBARD, humorist

Fighting is the only racket where you're almost guaranteed to end up as a bum.

> —ROCKY GRAZIANO, middleweight champion

When it's all finished and I write a book...the title will be "The Only Thing Square Was the Ring."

> —KEN NORTON, heavyweight champion

Bumper Snickers

KNIFE THE MAC.

> —Bumper sticker popular in Boston, where Red Sox manager John McNamara was sometimes unpopular

HONK IF YOU'VE BEEN MARRIED TO GEORGIA.

> —Bumper sticker in Los Angeles, referring to oft-wed Rams owner Georgia Frontiere

GO BRAVES—AND TAKE THE FALCONS WITH YOU.

> —A sentiment in Atlanta

BEAT ME, WHIP ME, MAKE ME LISTEN TO THE GIANTS.

—Bumper sticker in the San Francisco Bay Area

Bumper Stickers, Reaction to

I've never had so many people give me the finger on the [Los Angeles] freeways. It's non-stop.

—SAUL MARIASCHIN, Boston Celtic turned California businessman, revealing the perils of sporting a Celtic bumper sticker in Lakerland

Like Mariaschin, Chuck "The Rifleman" Connors was an early Celtic who became a Beverly Hills resident, but he wasn't as bold. "Are you nuts?" the actor asked when offered a similar sticker. "If I put on one of those things, I'd come out of the Forum and find four slashed tires."

Buttons

WE CAME. WE SAW. WE KICKED ASS.

—Button popular in Chicago after the Bears buried the Patriots, 46–10, in Super Bowl XX

Challenges

Don't forget, you still play this game with only one basketball.

—ARNOLD "RED" AUERBACH, Celtics general manager, upon hearing that the rival Lakers had acquired Wilt Chamberlain, sparking predictions that Boston's dynasty was over

Using only one basketball, the Celtics won the 1969 NBA title, their eleventh in thirteen seasons.

Cheating

They'll fire you for losing before they'll fire you for cheating.

—DARRYL ROGERS, football coach

I played a crooked game and I have lost.

—EDDIE CICOTTE, Chicago "Black Sox" pitcher, after being banned from baseball for life

Cheerleaders

Tell me. These women. Are they wayward?

—VIKTOR TIKHONOV, coach of the Soviet hockey team, after seeing the Dallas Cowboys cheerleaders in action

The NFL will have to adopt a hands-off policy on the cheerleaders.

—PETE ROZELLE, NFL commissioner

A Child's Garden of Curmudgeonliness

I've got to look in the paper to see how my favorite team did. Oh, rats...they won.

—OSCAR THE GROUCH, "Sesame Street"

A Civil Tongue

A lot of folks that ain't saying "ain't" ain't eating.

>—DIZZY DEAN, Hall of Fame pitcher turned broadcaster, responding to criticism of his fractured English

Coaches

A coach is often responsible to an irresponsible public.

>—BOB ZUPPKE, college football coach

I don't have an ulcer. I'm a carrier. I give them to other people.

>—BILL FITCH, NBA coach

I want my teams to have my personality—surly, obnoxious, and arrogant.

>—AL McGUIRE, basketball coach

The trouble with most coaches is they want to make the game too damn complicated.

>—BUDDY PARKER, NFL coach

There are only two kinds of coaches—those who have been fired and those who will be fired.

>—KEN LOEFFLER, basketball coach

A successful coach is one who is still coaching.

>—BEN SCHWARTZWALDER, football coach

I'd rather be a football coach. That way you only lose 11 games a year.

—ABE LEMONS, basketball coach

I sometimes feel like a dog trainer who has taken his little puppy and taught it everything...all manners, graces, and tricks. Then, just when the training is finished, the dog makes a puddle in the middle of the floor.

—ION TIRIAC, on coaching tennis' temperamental Ilie Nastase

Hotels have maids. Baseball teams have coaches.

—JOSÉ MARTINEZ, first-base coach, Kansas City Royals

First thing I got to do is learn how to chew tobacco and get the belly out. Got to have a big belly.

—RICHIE ALLEN, slugger turned coach, on the qualifications of being a coach

When you win, you're an old pro. When you lose, you're an old man.

—CHARLIE CONERLY, New York Giants quarterback

When I was losing, they called me nuts. When I was winning, they called me eccentric.

—AL McGUIRE, basketball coach

If you aren't fired with enthusiasm, you will be fired with enthusiasm.

> —VINCE LOMBARDI

Aren't all coaches *interim* coaches?

> —WREN BLAIR, Pittsburgh Penguins executive

Coaches Knocking Coaches

My father taught me never to interrupt.

> —KNUTE ROCKNE, explaining why he wouldn't ex-
> change words with Fielding "Hurry Up" Yost

College Football

A school without football is in danger of deteriorating into a medieval study hall.

> —VINCE LOMBARDI

It doesn't matter whether the NCAA stands for Nerds, Clods, and Androids, or Nitwits, Clowns, and Assholes. They all fit.

> —DAN JENKINS, novelist and humorist

One of the last great strongholds of genuine old-fashioned hypocrisy.

> —PAUL GALLICO, writer

Football—a sport that bears the same relation to education that bullfighting does to agriculture.

> —ELBERT HUBBARD, writer and editor

One of the greatest educational swindles ever perpetrated on American youth.

> —WHITNEY GRISWOLD, Yale president, on athletic scholarships

College football would be more interesting if the faculty played instead of the students—there would be an increase in broken arms, legs, and necks.

> —H. L. MENCKEN

Collegiate Suave

Gee, for a fat girl, you don't sweat much.

> —ALEX KARRAS, the future Detroit Lion and actor, when told to compliment an overweight dance partner at a college mixer

Competition

Anybody can win, unless there happens to be a second entry.

> —GEORGE ADE, humorist

I finished second.

> —FRITZIE ZIVIC, after a boxing defeat

Contact Sports

Football is not a contact sport. Football is a collision sport. Dancing is a contact sport.

>—DUFFY DAUGHERTY, coach

Cosell, Howard

If Howard Cosell was a sport, it would be roller derby.

>—JIMMY CANNON, columnist

Why are we honoring this man? Did we run out of human beings?

>—MILTON BERLE, at a roast for Cosell

In the next issue of *Cosmopolitan*, Howard Cosell will be the centerfold with his vital organ covered—his mouth.

>—BURT REYNOLDS, actor, sports enthusiast, and
>onetime centerfold

Sometimes I wish I was a dog and Howard was a tree.

>—MUHAMMAD ALI

Not while I'm alive.

>—IRVING RUDD, publicist, commenting on Howard
>Cosell's feeling that he is his own worst enemy

Crew

We ain't gonna have no sport where you sit down and go backwards.

>—FRANK HOWARD, athletic director, refusing to
>adopt crew in Clemson's athletic program

Cricket

I do not play cricket because it requires me to assume such indecent postures.

—OSCAR WILDE

Cross-Country Skiing

What you do at a cross-country ski race is look for the athlete whose nose has grown the longest icicle.

—DAN JENKINS, novelist and humorist

A Curmudgeon's Cheering Section

We want beer! We want beer!

—Philadelphia Athletics fans' enthusiastic 1931 welcome for President Herbert Hoover, noted Prohibition defender

That's putting the wood to it, Rabbit!

—A leather-lunged Boston fan to Walter "Rabbit" Maranville, after the little shortstop took a fastball on the skull, knocking him unconscious during the Boston Braves' 1914 "miracle" season

Steinbrenner sucks! Steinbrenner sucks!

> —Yankee Stadium chant after favorite Reggie Jackson homered in his first game back in New York wearing a California Angels' uniform

"It was just a big, unanimous thing that grew until it filled the park," the Yankees owner told reporters later. "I couldn't believe New York fans could use such language."

That comment made Yankee captain Graig Nettles wonder: "Where has he been all these years? Doesn't he come to the park? He must live in a dreamworld."

It's about the only fun time I had in the game.

> —RON GUIDRY, New York Yankees pitcher, commenting on that same cheer

Determination

Give me some scratching, diving, hungry ballplayers who come to kill you.

> —LEO DUROCHER

Diet

Ballplayers who are first into the dining room are usually last in the averages.

> —JIMMY CANNON, columnist

You mix two jiggers of Scotch to one jigger of Metrecal. So far I've lost five pounds and my driver's license.

> —ROCKY BRIDGES, humorous baseball veteran

After four days, you're hallucinating. After a week, you want to go out and find a grapefruit farmer and blow his head off.

> —FRANK ROBINSON, Baseball Hall of Famer, who lost 22 pounds on a grapefruit diet

I've seen self-induced vomiting, laxative abuse, excessive water and food deprivation, and even a self-induced bloody nose. If there's a way to lose weight, a wrestler will find it.

> —DON HERRMANN, assistant director of the Wisconsin Interscholastic Athletics Association

If it tastes good, spit it out.

> —ROGER MALTBIE, pro golfer, explaining how to lose 40 pounds

Nutrition makes me puke.

> —JIMMY PIERSALL, outfielder turned sportscaster

I'm a light eater. When it gets light, I start eating.

> —TOMMY JOHN, pitcher

Paris has three weaknesses: breakfast, lunch, and dinner.

> —ED WERDER, sportswriter, on San Francisco 49ers
> rookie lineman Bubba Paris, who weighed a reported
> 325 pounds

Fat guys need idols, too.

> —MICKEY LOLICH, six-foot, 250-pound pitcher

Divorce

It proves that no man can be a success in two national pastimes.

> —OSCAR LEVANT, on Joe DiMaggio's split
> with Marilyn Monroe

JOE DIMAGGIO STRIKES OUT

> —Headline over more than one newspaper account of
> the Joe and Marilyn divorce

How in the world can a woman say she deserves half of what I have because she stayed married to me for two years? She's never carried a football, she's never been hit once, or played with a hurt hamstring.

> —ERIC DICKERSON, NFL running back, on why
> he's evading marriage

My wife made me a millionaire. I used to have *three* million.

> —BOBBY HULL, Hockey Hall of Famer, on his former
> wife

It isn't a wife swap. It's a life swap.

> —MIKE KEKICH, trying to explain the spousal trans-
> action in which he and fellow New York Yankees
> pitcher Fritz Peterson exchanged wives

Divorce? No. Murder? Yes.

> —ANNE HAYES, wife of Ohio State football coach
> Woody Hayes, when asked if she'd ever considered
> divorce

Doctors

Gynecologist.

> —GEORGE FOREMAN, heavyweight champion,
> suggesting what Ferdinand "The Fight Doctor"
> Pacheco's real medical specialty might be

Dog Sled Racing

Those are not sled dogs!

> —Curmudgeonly complaint made by several 1991 Iditarod
> participants against John Suter, who entered a team
> of poodles in the 1,049-mile race across Alaska

In 1988 Suter's poodles finished a respectable thirty-eighth in a field of 52.

Drinking and Debauchery

Drinking is not a spectator sport.

> —JIM BROSNAN, pitcher turned author

If you drink, don't drive. Don't even putt.

> —DEAN MARTIN, who knows something about
> putting...and drinking

It depends on the length of the game.

> —MIKE "KING" KELLY, early baseball legend, when
> asked if he drank while playing baseball

There is much less drinking now than there was before 1927, because
I quit drinking on May 24, 1927.

> —WALTER "RABBIT" MARANVILLE, Hall of Fame
> shortstop

We're not going to drink any more this year.... Of course, we're not
going to drink any less, either.

> —DICK "THE MONSTER" RADATZ, ace fireman
> of the sixties, when asked in spring training about
> the Boston Red Sox's fun-loving reputation

Twenty, thirty beers before a game never hurt anybody.

> —LUCIEN DECHENE, hockey goalie

If any of my players don't take a drink now and then, they'll be gone. You don't play this game on ginger snaps.

>   —LEO DUROCHER

Either he was out very late or he was out very early.

>   —CASEY STENGEL, on the nocturnal habits of his insomniac pitcher, Don Larsen

The only thing he fears is sleep.

>   —JIMMY DYKES, who also managed Don Larsen

You couldn't disprove his story by the way he smelled.

>   —BRANCH RICKEY, St. Louis Cardinals general manager, on the return of one of his pitchers, Flint Rhem, who claimed he'd been kidnapped and forced to consume large amounts of liquor while locked in a room

I don't want anybody in bed by midnight. Everybody is to go out and get loaded.

>   —CHARLIE DRESSEN, Brooklyn Dodgers manager, advising his players after being swept by the Philadelphia Phillies

It worked. The Dodgers began winning again.

I never took the game home with me. I always left it in some bar.

>   —BOB LEMON, pitcher, manager, and Hall of Famer

Drinking as an Educational Experience

Yes. If you drink liquor, you won't have worms.

> —HACK WILSON, Hall of Fame outfielder, after his Chicago Cubs manager, Joe McCarthy, dropped a worm into his glass of gin and asked if it taught the outfielder anything

Duck Hunting

The perils of duck hunting are great, especially for the duck.

> —WALTER CRONKITE, anchorman

The Egomaniacs' Hall of Shame

I can lick any son of a bitch in the house.

> —JOHN L. SULLIVAN

When you're as great as I am, it's hard to be humble.

> —MUHAMMAD ALI

I never cease to amaze myself. I say this humbly.

> —DON KING, fight promoter

His greatest dream is to die in his own arms.

> —IRVING RUDD, fight promoter, on boxer Hector "Macho" Camacho

There never has been one like me before, and there will never be one like me again.

> —HOWARD COSELL, broadcaster

Young man, you have the question backwards.

> —BILL RUSSELL, Boston Celtics great, when asked how he would have fared playing in the pivot against Kareem Abdul-Jabbar

Nobody. *No*-body.

> —HARDY BROWN, notorious NFL hit man of the fifties, when asked if anyone could hit as hard as he

Son, they came to see old Jim play.

> —JIM THORPE, after leveling Knute Rockne in a collision of football immortals

Me—on instant replay.

> —DEREK SANDERSON, irrepressible Boston Bruin, when asked to name the best hockey player he ever saw

I'd pay to see me play.

> —ELVIN HAYES, Washington Bullet

Why can't they see the cold logic of it? I'm the straw that stirs the drink.

> —REGGIE JACKSON

I can't stand it, I'm so good.

> —TED WILLIAMS, in the batting cage

My only regret is that I can't sit in the stands and watch me pitch.

> —BO BELINSKY, pitcher

I just use it as a conversation piece. Like someone walking a cheetah down Forty-second Street would have a natural conversation piece.

> —ARNOLD SCHWARZENEGGER, bodybuilder, on his body

I was born for soccer, just as Beethoven was born for music.

> —PELÉ

Everybody is saying that I might be the most unpopular champion in the history of Wimbledon.... But what do I care? Because I am the champion.

> —JIMMY CONNORS, tennis champion

There's only one immortal player in the world today and it is Fischer. It's nice to be modest, but it's stupid not to tell the truth.

> —BOBBY FISCHER, the only American ever to win the chess world championship

Look at this face, ain't a mark on it. No other fighter ever looked this way. I am the greatest!

—MUHAMMAD ALI

Emotion

I'm a ballplayer, not an actor.

—JOE DiMAGGIO, explaining why he showed no emotion on the baseball diamond, even after hitting a home run

Emotion and Football

There was a lot of emotion at the Alamo, and nobody survived.

—RON MEYER, New England Patriots coach, on emotion being overrated in the NFL

Enemy Putdowns

Roy, you're the best player we've got on our team.

—CLIFF HARRIS, Dallas Cowboys safety, while patting the helmet of Pittsburgh Steelers kicker Roy Gerela after he missed a field-goal attempt in Super Bowl X

Terry Bradshaw couldn't spell cat if you spotted him the "c" and the "a."

> —THOMAS "HOLLYWOOD" HENDERSON, Dallas
> Cowboys linebacker, on the Pittsburgh Steelers
> quarterback.

After passing for 317 yards and four touchdowns against the Cowboys, Bradshaw suggested to reporters: "Go ask Henderson if I was dumb today."

Epitaphs

My epitaph is inescapable. It will read: "He sent a midget up to bat."

> —BILL VEECK, Baseball Hall of Fame owner and
> showman

If it was within my power, I would have inscribed on Ray Chapman's tombstone these words: "Here lies a victim of arrogance, viciousness, and greed."

> —TY COBB, in a note sent to Carl Mays via a Polo
> Grounds clubhouse boy moments before Mays took
> the mound for the first time after fatally beaning
> Chapman a week earlier

Equipment

I'll never strike out with that bat again!

> —BABE RUTH, angrily splintering his bat on dugout concrete after striking out mightily

The Eternal Optimism of Fans

Waiting for the Rams to win a Super Bowl is like leaving a porch light on for Jimmy Hoffa.

> —MILTON BERLE

Ethnic Athletics

Basketball's not my sport. Bocce ball's my sport. It's a gentleman's sport. You don't have to run around like an animal.

> —Father Guido Sarducci, comic television cleric

Ethnic Fouls

No, sir, unless it's a dumb Swede.

> —JIM CROWLEY, one of Notre Dame's "Four Horsemen," when coach Knute Rockne asked the halfback if there was "anything in the world dumber than a dumb Irishman"

When I finally get a nigger, I get the only one in the world who can't run.

> —CASEY STENGEL, on Elston Howard, the New York Yankees first black

I am pleased that God made my skin black, but I wish he had made it thicker.

> —CURT FLOOD, outfielder and baseball revolutionary

Excuses

I done it for the wife and kiddies.

> —EDDIE CICOTTE, Chicago "Black Sox" pitcher

I lost it in the sun.

> —BILLY LOES, Brooklyn Dodgers pitcher, after fumbling a grounder

Gee, Case, you had me on the bench so long my spikes got dulled on the concrete in the dugout.

> —OTTO HUBER, Boston Bees pinch runner, trying to explain to manager Casey Stengel why he had fallen on his face while rounding third—with what should have been the winning run in the 13th inning of a 1939 game

Poor Otto wasn't on the Boston bench much longer—soon cut by Stengel after only 11 games in the big leagues.

It was God's will.

> —BOB KNEPPER's reported reaction to surrendering
> a game-winning home run while a San Francisco
> Giants pitcher in 1980

Apparently it was also God's will that Knepper would do his pitching for the Houston Astros the following season.

I stood on the bag, just like you said. But I was a little nervous and was tapping my foot on the base. He must have gotten me between taps.

> —FRENCHY BORDAGARAY, Brooklyn Dodgers
> character, explaining to Casey Stengel how he got
> picked off despite the manager's order not to take a
> lead

My conscience is absolutely clear. It was an accident for which I am absolutely blameless. . . . It was the umpire's fault [for allowing a scuffed ball to be used]. A roughened spot on the ball, sometimes even a scratch, will make the ball do queer things. Umpires are instructed to throw out balls that have been roughened.

> —CARL MAYS, New York Yankees pitcher, on his
> "submarine pitch," which fractured the skull of
> Cleveland shortstop Ray Chapman in August 1920—
> the only fatal pitch in major league history

Veteran umpire Tommy Connolly claimed Mays was a master at disfiguring a ball to make it do strange things and get an edge in "trickery."

What self-respecting dog would be out at that hour?

> —ELLIS KINDER, Boston Red Sox pitcher with remark-
> able stamina on the field as well as off, adding a puckish
> postscript to his tale that he had crashed his car at
> 2:30 one morning in 1955 to avoid hitting a dog

Fairness

We wuz robbed.

> —JOE JACOBS, manager of Max Schmeling,
> when his narrowly outpointed boxer lost his
> heavyweight title to Jack Sharkey in a 15-
> round decision in 1932

Coach Lombardi is very fair. He treats us all like dogs.

> —HENRY JORDAN, veteran Green Bay Packer

Fame

I went through [baseball] life as a "player to be named later."

> —JOE GARAGIOLA, catcher turned broadcaster

Family Values

They shouldn't throw at me. I'm the father of five or six kids.

> —TITO FUENTES, San Francisco Giants infielder

I was led to believe I wasn't responsible for birth control. It was a communications situation there.

> —STEVE GARVEY, infielder, on how he managed to impregnate three women, none of them his wife, in a single year

It's hard to raise a family over the telephone.

> —DON SUTTON, pitcher

All right, you guys, look horny.

> —JIM BOUTON, to teammates as their plane taxied to the terminal after a long road trip

I take my wife with me because she's too ugly to kiss goodbye.

> —BUM PHILLIPS, Houston Oilers coach

Famous Last Words

Playing baseball for a living is like having a license to steal.

> —PETE ROSE, who lost that license abruptly in 1990 when he pleaded guilty to concealing income earned from his gambling winnings

You play shortstop, I'll do the pitching.

> —BOBO NEWSOM, to Joe Cronin after the Boston Red Sox player-manager trotted from his shortstop position to the mound with some pitching advice

The well-traveled Newsom, who changed uniforms 16 times in 20 major league seasons, did his pitching the next season for the St. Louis Browns, then the Devil's Island of the American League.

What for? He's dead.

> —DAVE BARRY, columnist, responding to the cry "Win one for the Gipper"

Yeah, Will Rogers.

> —DON JOE LOONEY, NFL halfback and character, when asked if he'd ever met a man he didn't like

No one would undergo a sex change for a reason as shallow as tennis.

> —DR. RENÉE RICHARDS, transsexual ophthalmologist and tennis professional

Nothing has the financial potential of women's basketball.

> —LARRY KOZLICKI, owner of the now defunct Nebraska Wranglers

All I had to do was keep turning left.

> —GEORGE ROBSON, winner of the 1946 Indianapolis 500

Fans

If they think we're stupid for playing this game, how stupid are they for watching us?

> —DENNY McLAIN, who won the Cy Young Award twice while pitching for the Tigers, on Detroit fans, whom he labeled "the biggest front-runners in the world"

They say Cubs fans are supposed to be behind you, and they're ripping everything we do. I hope we get hotter than [bleep] just to stuff those people. If they're the real Chicago Cubs fans, they can kiss my [bleeping] ass right downtown. And print that.

What am I supposed to do, let my players go out there and get destroyed every day and be quiet about it? Those [bleepers] don't even work. Eighty-five percent of the country is working and the other 15 percent is out here [Wrigley Field].

The 3,000 fans who show up here every day are the typical nickel-and-dime people who have nothing better to do with their lives than see our club destroyed. That's why they're at the game. It's a [bleeping] playground for them. Those fans are losers.

> —LEE ELIA, Chicago Cubs manager

Let 'em say what they're gonna say. I say he's gonna make it. When this season's over, I'm gonna walk down Michigan Boulevard and I'm gonna take my pants down and there's one-million guys that's gonna have to come over and kiss my ass.

> —ABE GIBRON, Chicago Bears coach, responding to fans' criticism of his quarterback choice

No crowds can frighten me.

> —TY COBB, after giving a defiant demonstration to 30,000 hostile New York Yankees fans, who responded to his dramatics with a chorus of curses followed by a near riot

The guy with the biggest stomach will be the first to take off his shirt at a baseball game.

> —GLENN DICKEY, columnist

Those fans. They've got the worst aim in the world.

> —TOMMY JOHN, New York Yankees pitcher, critiquing the irate fan who threw a bottle at umpire Ron Luciano—and missed

Fanimals.

> —DAVE WINFIELD, outfielder, referring to a specific breed of New York Yankees fan

Fuck you!

> —A message to Boston Red Sox outfielder Jimmy Piersall, scrawled on a hammer, one of many missiles hurled into center field during a game in Detroit in the fifties

Every obnoxious fan has a wife home who dominates him.

> —AL McGUIRE, basketball player and coach turned broadcaster

If they worked as hard at their jobs as I do at mine, this country wouldn't have the inflation problem it has now.

—MIKE MARSHALL, pitcher, on booing fans

You drive through New York and see people on the streets with no goal in life, nowhere to go. It's almost like people are miserable, and they want to bring you down to their level.

—KEVIN McREYNOLDS, New York Mets outfielder,
extolls the motivating power of supportive fans

Fans don't boo nobodies.

—REGGIE JACKSON

Nobody roots for Goliath.

—WILT CHAMBERLAIN

It is interesting about people that leave early from ball games. It's almost as if they came out to the game to see if they can beat the traffic home.

—LON SIMMONS, Oakland Athletics announcer

If they were losing in the old park, I'd stay. These rich people are just taking over. You see all these people in suits. You see these limousines. You see these suites. I'm just a regular steelworker. We're out of here.

—RALPH EDDERS, a displaced Chicago White Sox
fan, when the new Comiskey Park opened in 1991

The fan is everybody's sucker.

> —DOM PILEDGGI, founder of Sports Fans of America,
> a group fed up with overpriced tickets, cold hot dogs,
> and warm beer

If the crowds get any smaller they'll have to put fractions on the turnstiles.

> —MARK ROTH, New York Yankees traveling secretary

If the people don't want to come out to the park, nobody's going to stop 'em.

> —YOGI BERRA

Every crowd has a silver lining.

> —PHINEAS T. BARNUM, showman and curmud-
> geon, who also is credited with the truism "There's a
> sucker born every minute"

Fear

Everyone has some fear. A man who has no fear belongs in a mental hospital. Or on special teams.

> —WALT MICHAELS, New York Jets coach

Feats of Derring-do

I'm not a stunt man. I'm an explorer.

> —EVEL KNIEVEL, whose exploration of the Snake
> River Canyon nearly led him to the discovery of his
> final resting place

Femininity

If someone says it's not feminine, I say screw it.

—ROSEMARY CASALS, tennis pro

From the moment that the starting gate opens until my horse hits the wire, I'm a man competing against men. But by the time I get to the winner's circle, I'm reaching for my false eyelashes and I'm all girl.

—MARY BACON, jockey

It doesn't do girls any good to be stuck around together all the time. They become desexed, a terrible thing. It's easy to get caught up, not caring how you look, and lose the good points of one's sex.

—VIRGINIA WADE, tennis pro

I never saw an athletic girl that thought she was strong enough to do indoor work.

—FRANK McKINNEY "KIN" HUBBARD, humorist

She wore a tennis dress and eye makeup, but she had a deep voice and wasn't what you'd call feminine. I was thinking, is it a man or a woman? I was psyched out.

—ROBIN HARRIS, 20-year-old tennis player, describing
1976 La Jolla finals foe Renée Richards

When women kiss, it always reminds me of prize fighters shaking hands.

    —H. L. MENCKEN

Feuds

Two of sports' more likable guys didn't like each other. Red Smith, the first sports writer to win a Pulitzer Prize, and A. B. "Happy" Chandler, the governor and senator turned baseball commissioner (1945–51), feuded for years—Smith describing Chandler as a "clown," and Happy labeling Red "Whiskyhead Smith." Here is a sampling of what made their relationship great.

"They say he was the greatest writer," Chandler wrote in his autobiography. "To me he was just a damn drunk. Almost every time I encountered him he was soused to the ears. Red Smith was one of the commonest men I ever saw.

"The last time I saw him, he was in a cab in front of the Waldorf Astoria, drunk. I don't drink, and I don't associate with drunks."

And Smith once wrote in his *New York Herald Tribune* column: "Nothing that Happy Chandler did in his six unquiet years as baseball commissioner became him so well as his leave-taking."

The Finer Points of Baseball

I'm not sure what it means, but whenever the ball is not in play, somebody grabs his crotch.

    —PAULA BOUTON, the second Mrs. Jim Bouton

Fishing

A fishing rod is a stick with a worm on one end and a fool at the other.

—DR. SAMUEL JOHNSON

Fishing is a delusion entirely surrounded by liars in old clothes.

—DON MARQUIS, humorist

All men are equal before fish.

—HERBERT HOOVER, president who was hooked on fishing

It has always been my private conviction that any man who pits intelligence against a fish and loses has it coming.

—JOHN STEINBECK, novelist

"Angling" is the name given to fishing by people who can't fish.

—STEPHEN LEACOCK, author

An angler is a man who spends a lot of rainy days sitting around on the muddy banks of rivers doing nothing because his wife won't let him do it at home.

—*IRISH NEWS*

The biggest fish I caught got away.

> —EUGENE FIELD, poet

I would rather fish than eat, particularly eat fish.

> —COREY FORD, author and angler

Fishing, with me, has always been an excuse to drink in the daytime.

> —JIMMY CANNON, columnist

Florida's alright if you can keep from catching a sailfish and going to the expense of having it mounted.

> —FRANK McKINNEY "KIN" HUBBARD,
> humorist

There is no use in walking five miles to fish when you can depend on being just as unsuccessful near home.

> —MARK TWAIN

Fixes

He's throwing games on me!

> —FRANK CHANCE, 1915 New York Yankees
> manager, on Hal Chase, a few days before the star
> first baseman was virtually given away to the Chicago
> White Sox

At least two others who managed Chase—Christy Mathewson and George Stallings—also accused Chase of throwing games.

He had a corkscrew brain.

> —JIM PRICE, *New York Press* sports editor, describing first baseman Hal Chase, often referred to as the most crooked player in the history of baseball—and widely accused of masterminding the 1919 "Black Sox" scandal, on which he won a bundle

They can't come back. The doors are closed to them for good. The most scandalous chapter in baseball history is closed.

> —KENESAW MOUNTAIN LANDIS, baseball commissioner, ruling that the eight accused "Black Sox" fixers of the 1919 World Series were forever banished despite the court's "not guilty" verdict

Food

I've often wondered what goes into a hot dog. Now I know and I wish I didn't.

> —WILLIAM ZINSSER, writer, editor, and teacher

Food Comes Up a Second Time

Thank God! They electrocuted the chef!

>   —JIMMY CANNON, columnist, when the lights flickered during a baseball writers' dinner

Football

This is a game for madmen.

>   —VINCE LOMBARDI

Football is a sensible game—but it is surrounded by crazy people.

>   —LOU LITTLE, Columbia coach

Tackling is football. Running is track.

>   —EMLEN TUNNELL, Hall of Fame safety

The football season is like pain. You forget how terrible it is until it seizes you again.

>   —SALLY QUINN, journalist and author

Pro football is like nuclear warfare. There are no winners, only survivors.

>   —FRANK GIFFORD, Hall of Fame halfback turned broadcaster

Football is the only game you come into with a semblance of intelligence and end up a babbling moron.

> —MIKE ADAMLE, fullback turned broadcaster

In pro football you need to be around 30 years to get 10 years of enjoyment.

> —BOB TISCH, New York Giants co-owner, stating a fact most Giants fans already know

Football is more than just a game. It is a potential opportunity to see a live person lying on the ground with a bone sticking out of his leg, while the fans, to show their appreciation, perform "the wave."

> —DAVE BARRY, humorist

Football as a Religious Experience

What do Jimmy Swaggart and Saints coach Jim Mora have in common? They can get 60,000 people under one roof screaming "Jesus Christ!"

> —STEVE BRIER, reporter

Football Fans

The more violent the body contact of the sports you watch, the lower your class.

> —PAUL FUSSELL, author

The average football fan is a college graduate with an eighth grade education.

> —ANDY ROONEY, humorist

He'll scream from the 60th row of bleachers that you missed a marginal call in the center of the interior line and then won't be able to find his car in the parking lot.

> —JIM TUNNEY, referee, on some NFL fans

Football is a game designed to keep coal miners off the streets.

> —JIMMY BRESLIN, columnist and author

Football Officials

Officials are the only guys who can rob you and then get a police escort out of the stadium.

> —RON BOLTON, NFL defensive back

Football Officials, Shortsighted

I'd be an official, just like you.

> —FRED ARBANAS, blind in one eye, responding to an official who asked what the Kansas City Chiefs tight end would do if he lost sight in the other eye

Stevie Wonder could have seen I didn't have that ball.

> —MARK CLAYTON, Miami Dolphins receiver, after officials ruled that he had fumbled the ball—not dropped the pass

The officials blew this one. They're more powerful than the Pope. Tomorrow they'll go back to their $12-a-day jobs and there's nothing we can do about it.

> —JOHN McKAY, Tampa Bay Bucs coach

During the week, I practice law. On Sundays, I *am* the law.

> —TOMMY BELL, attorney and NFL referee

Football Strategy

I find the shortest distance to the ball carrier and try to time my arrival in ill humor.

> —EUGENE "BIG DADDY" LIPSCOMB, NFL defensive tackle and legend

Football Weather

It was an ideal day for football—too cold for the spectators and too cold for the players.

> —RED SMITH, columnist

Foxhunting

The English country gentleman galloping after a fox—the unspeakable in full pursuit of the uneatable.

> —OSCAR WILDE

Front-Office Backhands

Leo Durocher is a man with an infinite capacity to take a bad situation and make it immediately worse.

> —BRANCH RICKEY, baseball legend, lipping off about "The Lip"

Gambling

It is the child of avarice, the brother of iniquity, and the father of mischief.

> —GEORGE WASHINGTON, who was the father of something else

The urge to gamble is so universal and its practice is so pleasurable that I assume it must be evil.

> —HEYWOOD HALE BROUN, journalist and broadcaster

A racetrack is a place where windows clean people.

—DANNY THOMAS, comic

The race is not always to the swift, nor the battle to the strong, but that's the way to bet.

—DAMON RUNYON, author

The only man who makes money following the races is the one who does so with a broom and shovel.

—ELBERT HUBBARD, writer and editor

My biggest crime is stupidity.

—DENNY McLAIN, two-time Cy Young Award winner, during his gambling difficulties, which would land him in prison

I should have stood in bed.

—JOE JACOBS, fight manager, after getting out of a sickbed to attend a thirties World Series game—and betting on the losing team

Getting Fired

You're goddamn right I was fired.

—CASEY STENGEL after the 70-year-old manager was "retired" two days after losing the

seventh game of the 1960 World Series, having
piloted the Yankees to 10 pennants and
seven world championships in his 12 seasons
as their manager

If you don't win, you're going to get fired. If you do win, you've only put off the day you're going to be fired.

—LEO DUROCHER

Behind every fired football coach stands a college president.

—JOHN McKAY, USC football coach

All I know is, I pass people on the street these days and they don't know whether to say hello or goodbye.

—BILLY MARTIN, often-fired Yankees manager

I feel like I've been freed from slavery.

—DARRELL JACKSON, pitcher, upon being released
by the Minnesota Twins after five years of hard labor
in Calvin Griffith's vineyard

The First Amendment doesn't give you carte blanche to knock your employer.

—JIM KENSIL, New York Jets president, after waiving
linebacker Bob Martin for mouthing off about the
team's management

Winning is the name of the game. The more you win the less you get fired.

—ARMAND "BEP" GUIDOLIN, hockey coach

Getting replaced by Bill Curry, that really bothered me. It's kind of like having your wife run off with Don Knotts.

—PEPPER RODGERS, after being let go as Georgia Tech football coach in favor of Curry

Gimme the Ball

See those people up there? Those people came to see Big Ed score. But Big Ed can't score if Big Ed doesn't shoot the ball. And Big Ed can't shoot the ball if Big Ed doesn't have the ball.

So let's pass the goddamn ball to Big Ed!

—ED SADOWSKI, the Boston Celtics' first all-league center, calling a timeout to scold teammates in 1948

Goals

All I want out of life is that when I walk down the street folks will say, "There goes the greatest hitter who ever lived."

—TED WILLIAMS

My goal in life is to be on "Cheers," sitting next to Normie, talking to Sam Malone.

—DAVE LAPOINT, pitcher

I'd like to be the first male reporter who tries to get into the women's tennis locker room.

—GEORGE STEINBRENNER

Golf

An attempt to place a small, little sphere in a slightly larger hole with utensils totally unsuited to the task.

—WOODROW WILSON, president and golfer

Golf was, I should say offhand, the most useless game ever devised to waste the time and try the spirit of man.

—WESTBROOK PEGLER, columnist

Golf is a good walk spoiled.

—MARK TWAIN

Golf is an expensive way of playing marbles.

—G. K. CHESTERTON, author

Cow-pasture pool.

> —O. K. BOVARD, journalist, describing golf

A game in which you claim the privileges of age, and retain the playthings of childhood.

> —DR. SAMUEL JOHNSON

Golf . . . a young man's vice and an old man's penance.

> —IRVIN S. COBB, humorist

What, after all, is a golf course except a glorified lawn perforated by 18 holes?

> —WITOLD RYBCZYNSKI, author

Golf is mostly a game of failures.

> —TOMMY AARON, pro golfer

Golf is not a sport. Golf is men in ugly pants walking.

> —ROSIE O'DONNELL, comic

It enables me to dress like an idiot.

> —HUEY LEWIS, rock star, on the benefits of golf

The only way to get hurt playing golf is to get struck by lightning.

> —TED WILLIAMS, who once despised the sport

If you can't break 85 you have no business on the golf course. If you can break 85 you probably have no business.

> —*THE OLD FARMER'S ALMANAC*

Eighteen holes of match or medal play will teach you more about your foe than will 18 years of dealing with him across a desk.

> —GRANTLAND RICE, sportswriter

[Golf is] a game you play with your worst enemy.

> —FINLEY PETER DUNNE, humorist

It took me 17 years to get 3,000 hits in baseball. I did it in one afternoon at the golf course.

> —HANK AARON, a slugger on both fields of dreams

Any game where a man 60 can beat a man 30 ain't no game.

> —BURT SHOTTON, baseball manager

If you watch a game, it's fun. If you play it, it's recreation. If you work at it, it's golf.

> —BOB HOPE

Golf is essentially an exercise in masochism conducted out of doors.

> —PAUL O'NEIL, journalist

Golf is not a funeral, though both can be very sad affairs.

—BERNARD DARWIN, writer

Golf and Politics

If there is any larceny in a man, golf will bring it out.

—PAUL GALLICO, writer

Scorecard.

—Secret Service code name for Vice President Dan Quayle

If I had my way, any man guilty of golf would be ineligible for any office of trust in the United States.

—H. L. MENCKEN

Rail splitting produced an immortal president in Abraham Lincoln; but golf, with 29 courses, hasn't even produced a good A-Number 1 Congressman.

—WILL ROGERS

Yes. A lot more golfers beat me.

—DWIGHT EISENHOWER, president and golfer, when asked if his game had changed any since leaving the White House

A Golf Tip

Never go out on the golf course and beat the president.

> —LYNDON JOHNSON, another president
> and golfer

Another Golf Tip

The Grip: Get a firm grip on your credit cards; otherwise you will have to buy all of the drinks and lunch. Rich guys never pay for shit.

> —DAN JENKINS, novelist and humorist

Gore

Blood! That's what I want—blood!

> —PERCY HAUGHTON, coach of Harvard's pre–
> World War I football powerhouses, telling his
> Crimson team what he expected of them on a
> given Saturday

Gratitude

When we won the championship, all the married guys on the club had to thank their wives for putting up with all the stress and strain all season. I had to thank half the broads in New York.

> —JOE NAMATH, New York Jets quarterback and
> bachelor

Great Comebacks

If you're so smart, let's see you get out of the Army.

> —CASEY STENGEL's reply to a soldier who had criticized his managing of the lowly Boston Bees (*née* Braves)

He Said, She Said

Well, girls . . . shall we go?

> —DANA X. BIBLE, Texas A&M football coach, jabbing his players at halftime

He should be wearing a skirt, not a football uniform.

> —JOHN HANNAH, Pro Football Hall of Famer, on New England Patriots teammate Tony Eason

Wimps and fairies.

> —MIKE GREENWELL's description of his 1989 Boston Red Sox teammates after just three (two half-heartedly) left the dugout to defend pitcher Mike Smithson against a charge to the mound by Rafael Palmeiro and the entire Texas Rangers bench

Asked about Greenwell's portrayal, Sox manager Joe Morgan replied during a live television interview: "A pretty good assessment."

The High Cost of a Perfect Lawn

If the Astrodome is the Eighth Wonder of the World, then the rent is the ninth.

> —BUD ADAMS, Houston Oilers owner, when
> Houston's indoor stadium opened

Hitting

If there was ever a man born to be a hitter, it was me.

> —TED WILLIAMS, probably baseball's best hitter ever

I'd rather hit than have sex.

> —REGGIE JACKSON, who wasn't bad either

Hockey

I went to a fight the other night and a hockey game broke out.

> —RODNEY DANGERFIELD, comic

A hard rubber disk that hockey players strike when they can't hit one another.

> —JIMMY CANNON, columnist, defining a puck

Most citizens living south of the Frozen-Pond parallel can caricature hockey as wrestling on skates performed by small-town louts.

—GEORGE VECSEY, columnist

Hockey players are like mules. They have no fear of punishment and no hope of reward.

—EMORY JONES, general manager of St. Louis Arena

Hockey Fans

The crowd at the Garden put me at ease instantly. For two hours or so, I felt that all of the people in the city who might otherwise have been breaking out store-front windows, mugging old ladies, or knocking off delis were there with me.

—DAN JENKINS, humorist, reacting to the
crowd drawn by the New York Rangers

Hockey Fights

Hockey's the only place where a guy can go nowadays and watch two white guys fight.

—FRANK DEFORD, writer

If you can't beat 'em in the alley, you can't beat 'em on the ice.

> —CONN SMYTHE, Toronto Maple Leafs general
> manager

If hockey fights were faked, you'd see me in more of them.

> —ROD GILBERT, veteran New York Ranger

You know a guy [opponent] has a broken wrist, you hammer him there a few times and you don't have much trouble with him for the rest of the night. It's nothing personal.

> —PUNCH IMLACH, NHL coach

I figure anybody hits you, you should hit him back. Isn't that the way the game's supposed to be played?

> —BOBBY CLARKE, veteran Philadelphia Flyer

When a player enters an arena, he is consenting to a great number of what otherwise might be regarded as assaults. The game of hockey could not possibly be played unless those engaged in it were willing to accept these assaults.

> —JUDGE M. J. FITZPATRICK commenting on a
> near-fatal 1970 stick-swinging between Ted Green of
> the Boston Bruins and Wayne Maki of the St. Louis
> Blues

Hockey and Politics

She doesn't pay me anything. I pay her. Besides, what position can she play?

> —HAROLD BALLARD, Toronto Maple Leafs owner, explaining why he removed Queen Elizabeth's picture to make room for more seats at Maple Leaf Gardens

Horseracing

Thirty tons a day.

> —BILL VEECK, Baseball Hall of Fame owner and showman—and onetime president of Suffolk Downs—on the ultimate end product of horseracing ... and the title of a book on his Boston racetrack experience co-authored with Ed Linn

Horsewomen

Eight fillies on eight fillies. I'd like to put eight maidens on eight maidens, but I don't think I'd be able to fill the race.

> —BILL VEECK, between baseball jobs, explaining his first racing attraction as boss of Suffolk Downs in 1969—an all-female Lady Godiva Handicap, exploiting the emergence of female jockeys

The only one I ever heard of to make a historical contribution was Lady Godiva.

> —SAMMY RENICK, jockey, on his female colleagues

My mount that day was a horse in foal. I couldn't help but think about those fans betting on a pregnant horse ridden by a pregnant jockey. The four of us finished last.

> —MARY BACON, jockey, recalling a race she rode a week before giving birth

A horse doesn't know whether the rider on his back wears a dress or pants away from the track.

> —DIANE CRUMP, a female jockey pioneer

Humiliation

He really enjoyed demeaning people.

> —JIMMY PIERSALL, after going from outfield to the front office, on former employer Charles O. Finley

He told me he needed lots of work, so I gave it to him.

> —MILLER HUGGINS, New York Yankees manager, after gleefully letting Carl Mays, whom he hated, pitch the full nine innings of a 13–0 loss in 1923

After the game Yankees shortstop Everett Scott sympathized with Mays, who hadn't pitched for some time prior to the pounding.

"In all my years in baseball, I've never seen anything so rotten as this," Scott said. "But don't worry. The worm will turn. It always does."

"A worm is the same on all sides," Mays replied. "Especially that worm."

Hunting

When a man wants to murder a tiger he calls it sport. When a tiger wants to murder him he calls it ferocity.

—GEORGE BERNARD SHAW

Wild animals never kill for sport. Man is the only one [for] whom the torture and death of his fellow creatures is amusing in itself.

—J. A. FROUDE, historian

Detested sport/That owes its pleasure to another's pain.

—WILLIAM COWPER, poet

I Am Not a Crook

They got outlaws playing the game, bank robbers, all kinds of things. Murderers, rapists, all kinds of [bleep].

I ain't done none of that. I can pitch a baseball and nobody will let me do it.

—DENNIS "OIL CAN" BOYD, 32-year-old
unemployed pitcher in spring 1992, sug-

gesting a hands-off policy against him by
baseball teams—and ignoring his 2–7,
6.68 ERA statistics for the Texas Rangers
the previous season

Injuries

Hurt is in your mind.

> —HARRY LOMBARDI, to son Vince, who one day
> would vigorously practice that philosophy as a
> football coaching immortal

If you can walk, you can run.

> —VINCE LOMBARDI, amplifying on his mind-over-
> matter philosophy

It's just ice. That doesn't mean they're hurt.

> —BILL PARCELLS, New York Giants coach, explain-
> ing the bags worn around knees and elbows after the
> average football game

Don't touch him! Let him lay there. It might drive some sense into the
son of a bitch.

> —CASEY STENGEL, Boston Braves manager, after
> Max West was KO'd by a line drive while drinking
> from a dugout water fountain, minutes after making
> a colossal blunder on the field

Like someone slapping jello.

> —RON LUCIANO, former umpire, describes the sound of Ken Tatum's fastball connecting with Paul Blair's head

WHAM! WHAM! WHAM!...WHAM! WHAM! WHAM!
WHAM! WHAM! WHAM!...POP! POP!

> —MUHAMMAD ALI

I learned a long time ago that minor surgery is when they do the operation on someone else, not you.

> —BILL WALTON, basketball center and surgery survivor

My knees look like they lost a knife fight with a midget.

> —E. J. HOLUB, linebacker, after a dozen knee operations

I don't want any doctor building a swimming pool with my knee.

> —STEVE HOWE, pitcher, passing on surgery

Fractured, hell! The damn thing's broken!

> —DIZZY DEAN, one-of-a-kind pitcher and linguist, on his hurtin' toe

When you win, nothing hurts.

> —JOE NAMATH, Hall of Fame quarterback

First triple I ever had.

> —LEFTY GOMEZ, onetime star pitcher, on triple-bypass surgery

My problem's, uh, behind me now.

> —GEORGE BRETT, batting champion, after hemorrhoid surgery

I wake up in the morning, take one look in the mirror and immediately start limping.

> —MICKEY HATCHER, outfielder

You never know with these psychosomatic injuries. You have to take your time with them.

> —JIM PALMER, Hall of Fame pitcher

Disabled List, U.S.A.

> —DICK YOUNG, baseball writer, suggesting the home address of Dave Kingman

Inspiration from the Locker Room

Stay close in the early innings, and I'll think of something.

> —CHARLIE DRESSEN, manager of the
> Brooklyn Dodgers' "Boys of Summer"

Stick it in his ear.

> —LEO DUROCHER's frequent advice to his pitchers

Interview Questions from Hell

So, tell me, Pete—did they have casino night for you once a week when you were in prison?

> —"STUTTERING JOHN" MELENDEZ, man-on-
> the-street for the "Howard Stern Show," to Pete
> Rose

Did you ever accidently fart in the catcher's face?

> —Same interviewer to Ted Williams, who responded
> with a terse "Who the hell are you?"

Yeah, Gary Carter's. Ask him.

> —KEITH HERNANDEZ, New York Met, gamely
> responding to the same question

It's How You Play the Game

Why they call a fellow who keeps losing all the time a good loser gets me.

> —FRANK McKINNEY "KIN" HUBBARD, humorist

Show me a good loser and I'll show you a loser.

> —ARNOLD "RED" AUERBACH, basketball Hall of Fame coach

Show me a gracious loser and I'll show you a perennial loser.

> —O.J. SIMPSON, Hall of Fame halfback

Show me a gracious loser and I'll show you a failure.

> —KNUTE ROCKNE

Show me a good loser in professional sports and I'll show you an idiot.

> —LEO DUROCHER

There never was a champion who to himself was a good loser. There's a vast difference between a good sport and a good loser.

> —EARL "RED" BLAIK, West Point football coach

If there's a good loser in boxing, I'd like to fight him every week.

> —GENE FULLMER, middleweight champion

All quitters are good losers.

> —BOB ZUPPKE, college football coach

Good losers get into the habit of losing.

> —GEORGE ALLEN, NFL coach

Grantland Rice, the great sportswriter, once said, "It's not whether you win or lose, it's how you play the game." Well, Grantland Rice can go to hell as far as I'm concerned.

> —GENE AUTRY, Hollywood singing cowboy turned California Angels owner

It's not whether you win or lose, but who gets the blame.

> —BLAINE NYE, Dallas Cowboys lineman

If there is such a thing as a good loser, then the game is crooked.

> —BILLY MARTIN, baseball manager

I knew a good loser once. He was queer.

> —BARRY GOLDWATER, politician

Jackson, Reggie

There isn't enough mustard in the whole world to cover that hot dog.

> —DAROLD KNOWLES, pitcher, on onetime Oakland A's teammate

Jackson, Reggie and George Steinbrenner

One's a born liar and the other's convicted.

> —BILLY MARTIN, on-again, off-again New York Yankees manager in a double-barreled blast that got him fired—again

Jockeying Around

The horse weighs 1,000 pounds and I weigh 95. I guess I'd better get him to cooperate.

> —STEVE CAUTHEN, jockey

Lincoln went down in history as "Honest Abe" but he never was a jockey. If he had been a jockey he might have gone down as just "Abe."

> —WILL ROGERS

Jogging

It's unnatural for people to run around city streets unless they are thieves or victims. It makes people nervous to see someone running. I know that when I see someone running on my street, my instincts tell me to let the dog out after him.

> —MIKE ROYKO, columnist

If the poor overweight jogger only knew how far he had to run to work off the calories in a crust of bread he might find it better in terms of pound per mile to go to a massage parlor.

—DR. CHRISTIAAN BARNARD, heart surgeon

Jogging is very beneficial. It's good for your legs and your feet. It's also very good for the ground. It makes it feel needed.

—SNOOPY

The Joy of Baseball

I loved the game, I loved the competition. But I never had any fun. All hard work, all the time.

—CARL YASTRZEMSKI, Hall of Famer,
reflecting on his career during his
final Boston Red Sox season

Knocking the Barkeep

Who read it to you?

—BOB CONSIDINE to Toots Shor, when the New
York saloon keeper complimented the writer
on that day's column

Leadership

You gotta be a prick!

> —GEORGE STEINBRENNER's often-
> repeated credo to his New York
> Yankees management team

Sure I'm a dictator—a benevolent dictator, but a dictator all the same. There's room for only one boss and that's me.

> —ARNOLD "RED" AUERBACH

This is a dictatorship, and I'm the dictator.

> —AL DAVIS, pro football owner and former coach

I'm not into that business of being relevant to kids. I'm not playing on their team; they're playing on mine. We have certain ways of acting here. My kids are not going to come in here and say "Hey, baby." It doesn't make you less of a man to have respect for people.

> —JOHN THOMPSON, Georgetown basketball coach

I don't communicate with players. I tell them what to do. I don't understand the meaning of communication.

> —PAUL RICHARDS, during his second tour as
> Chicago White Sox manager, when asked if he in-
> tended to initiate dialogue with one of his players

I'm not buddy-buddy with the players. If they need a buddy, let them buy a dog.

> —WHITEY HERZOG, baseball manager

I'm the only chief. All the rest are Indians.

> —DICK WILLIAMS, rookie manager, upon taking the reins of the 1967 Boston Red Sox, relieving Carl Yastrzemski of his captaincy and eliminating the title

License Plates

Don Buddin should have E-6 on his automobile license plate.

> —CLIF KEANE writing in the *Boston Globe* about the Boston Red Sox' error-prone shortstop of the fifties

Buddin didn't take the suggestion in the best of humor. He had to be restrained the next time Keane showed up in the Fenway Park locker room.

Life in the Little Leagues

Teaching baseball to five-year-olds is like trying to organize a bunch of earthworms.

> —DOROTHY McCONNELL, writer

For the parent of a Little Leaguer, a baseball game is simply a nervous breakdown divided into innings.

> —EARL WILSON, columnist

It keeps the kids out of the house.

> —YOGI BERRA, on the benefits of Little League Baseball

[Little League] takes the fun out of athletics at an early age.

> —DR. BENJAMIN SPOCK, on why he feels Little League Baseball should be abolished

Come on, Leroy, as long as you've got your thumb in your mouth, throw a spitball.

> —FLIP WILSON, comic, coaching his son

Get your shit over the plate. Get your damned shit over.

> —PETEY ROSE, age three, son of Pete, pinpointing the spot where he wants a pitch

Locker-Room Philosophy

I like my players to be married and in debt. That way you motivate them.

> —ERNIE BANKS, as a minor league instructor

Ain't no sense in worrying about things you got control over, 'cause if you got control over them, ain't no sense worrying. And there ain't no sense worrying about things you got no control over, 'cause if you got no control over them, ain't no sense worrying about them.

> —MICKEY RIVERS, New York Yankees outfielder and philosopher

You can lead a horse to water, but you can't stick his head in it.

> —PAUL OWENS, Philadelphia Phillies manager

If they try to knock you over, hit the motherfucker right in the mouth with the ball.

> —BILLY MARTIN, second baseman turned manager, advising his infielders how to protect themselves around the keystone sack

Losers

The man who can accept defeat and take his salary is a thief.

> —GEORGE ALLEN, NFL coach

Losers, Sore

I'll follow the S.O.B. to the ends of the earth. Everywhere he turns he'll see my shadow.

> —JIMMY CONNORS, after losing to Bjorn Borg at Wimbledon in 1978

Losing

Losing is the great American sin.

> —JOHN R. TUNIS, writer

This team has shown me ways to lose I couldn't believe. You've got to look up and down the bench and say, "Can't anyone here play this game?"

> —CASEY STENGEL, on his early, hapless Amazin' Mets

Last year wasn't all that bad. We led the league in flu shots.

> —BILL FITCH, coach, describing his early Cleveland Cavaliers

It's a lonesome walk to the sidelines, especially when thousands of people are cheering your replacement.

> —FRAN TARKENTON, quarterback and scrambler

They say I teach brutal football, but the only thing brutal about football is losing.

> —BEAR BRYANT, Alabama football coach

If a tie is like kissing your sister, losing is like kissing your grandmother with her teeth out.

> —GEORGE BRETT, batting champion

No one knows what to say in the loser's room.

>　　　—MUHAMMAD ALI

The game was not as close as the score indicates.

>　　　—DUFFY DAUGHERTY, Michigan State coach,
>　　　reviewing his football team's 49–14 loss

A Low Blow

Due to a typing error, Governor Michael Dukakis was incorrectly identified in the third person as Mike Tyson.

>　　　—A correction in the *Fitchburg-Leominster*
>　　　[Massachusetts] *Sentinel and Enterprise*

Loyalty

I'm the most loyal player money can buy.

>　　　—DON SUTTON, a pitcher who appreciated
>　　　free-agency

The Lure of the Professional Athlete

Who wants to go with a guy who's got two bad knees and a quick release?

>　　　—CONNIE STEVENS, actress, on popular
>　　　quarterback and bachelor Joe Namath

The Managerial Touch

You *thought*? With what?

> —JOHN McGRAW, to any of his players silly
> enough to begin a sentence with the
> words "I thought..."

You're full of shit, and I'll tell you why....

> —CASEY STENGEL's frequent rebuttal

Why, Carl, are you still with the team?

> —MILLER HUGGINS, New York Yankees manager,
> responding in front of a dugout full of reporters to
> Carl Mays' question "Hug, why don't you let me
> pitch?"

Bobby Brown reminds me of a fellow who's been hitting for 12 years
and fielding for one.

> —CASEY STENGEL, on his New York Yankees third
> baseman, Bobby Brown, who became American
> League president

Mike Anderson's limitations are limitless.

> —DANNY OZARK's assessment of his Philadelphia
> Phillies outfielder

Big leaguers? Bah! You couldn't even beat a bunch of females.

> —GEORGE STALLINGS to his last-place Boston
> Braves after they had lost an exhibition game to a
> minor league team in mid-season, 1914

Inspired, the "Miracle Braves" caught fire and not only won the pennant by 10 1/2 games, but swept Connie Mack's defending champion Philadelphia Athletics in the World Series.

Managers

A baseball manager is a necessary evil.

> —SPARKY ANDERSON, who has done his part
> with the Cincinnati Reds and Detroit Tigers

Managing is a lonely, difficult job. It's not fun. It's a nightmare. But I enjoy it.

> —MAURY WILLS, Seattle Mariners manager

The way things are going for me, if I'd buy a pumpkin farm they'd cancel Halloween.

> —BILLY GARDNER, Minnesota Twins manager

If you start worrying about the people in the stands, before too long you're in the stands with them.

> —TOMMY LASORDA, Los Angeles Dodgers
> manager

Don't cut my throat. I may want to do that myself later.

> —CASEY STENGEL, to his barber

A man with a license to make a living while committing vagrancy.

> —JIMMY CANNON, columnist, describing a fight manager

When I get through managing, I'm going to open a kindergarten.

> —BILLY MARTIN, manager

Marathon Madness

I don't discriminate against women. They're just not allowed to run in my race.

> —JOHN "JOCK" SEMPLE, Boston Marathon co-director

When I was first running marathons, we were sailing on a flat earth. We were afraid we'd get big legs, grow moustaches, not get boyfriends, not be able to have babies. Women thought that something would happen to them, that they'd break down or turn into men. . . .

> —KATHY SWITZER, who in 1967 became the first numbered woman to run in the Boston Marathon— unofficially

Knowing that women had been excluded from the Boston race, Kathy Switzer registered simply as "K. Switzer" and pinned number 261 to her sweater. When Jock Semple spotted her from the press bus, the race codirector disembarked and lunged at the runner.

"Get . . . out . . . of . . . my . . . race! You're not supposed to be in my race!" the crusty Scot burred.

Unknown to Semple, Kathy's burly boyfriend, Tom Miller, was running alongside. He responded to Semple's assault by all but leveling him with a running block that was captured by cameramen and published worldwide under the caption "The Great Shoving Match."

There was a happy ending. Kathy and Jock literally kissed and made up. And in 1972 Semple and Switzer posed happily for pictures when he presented her a trophy for placing third among female finishers in that year's marathon—the first time the race welcomed women.

"Hell, I've been for women all along," Semple would recall before his death in 1988. "But all people will ever remember is that I'm the guy who tossed that girl out of the Boston Marathon."

Marriage

Marriage is a great institution—to a lot of women.

—RON LUCIANO, umpire turned author

For most ballplayers, all getting married means is that now they have to *hide* their datebooks.

—DON KOWET, writer

It's got to be better than rooming with Joe Page.

> —JOE DiMAGGIO on the advent of what would be his nine-month marriage to Marilyn Monroe

Marshall arrived bag and baggage.

> —SHIRLEY POVICH, *Washington Post* columnist, on the return to Washington of Redskins owner George Preston Marshall and his bride, actress Corinne Griffith, from their honeymoon

My wife doesn't care what I do when I'm away as long as I don't have fun.

> —LEE TREVINO, pro golfer

Explaining to your wife why *she* needs a penicillin shot for *your* kidney infection.

> —MIKE HEGAN, first baseman, suggesting the toughest thing in baseball

My wife accused me the other day of loving baseball more than I loved her. I told her she was right, but that I did love her more than football and basketball.

> —TOMMY LASORDA, Los Angeles Dodgers manager

If it weren't for the money, I'd retire and go caddie for my wife.

>   —RAY KNIGHT, third baseman and husband of pro
>   golfer Nancy Lopez

The most positive thing that came out of my marriage was that I learned to appreciate the traveling.

>   —RON LUCIANO

She's a plain kid. She'd give up the business if I asked her. She'd quit the movies in a minute.

>   —JOE DiMAGGIO on his wife, Marilyn Monroe, who
>   ultimately gave him up instead

What husband isn't?

>   —ANNE HAYES, wife of Ohio State football coach
>   Woody Hayes, responding to a heckler who labeled
>   her husband "a fathead"

Marriage, Sports, and Money

This club is a lot of fun, like my wife. But there's no profit in either one.

>   —RAY KROC, San Diego Padres owner

I never realized how short a month is until I started paying alimony.

>   —HARRY CARAY, baseball announcer

Mental Health

He showed it was a game, so they locked him up.

> —ABBIE HOFFMAN, Yippie, on Jimmy Piersall, once
> hospitalized in a mental institution while a
> Boston Red Sox player

Cuckoo . . . cuckoo . . . cuckoo. . . .

> —DICK WILLIAMS, an all-star bench jockey, needling
> batter Jimmy Piersall

Probably the best thing that ever happened to me was going nuts.

> —JIMMY PIERSALL, who was propelled into national
> prominence by the autobiography and movie detail-
> ing his breakdown

Who needs the psychiatrist now?

> —DENNIS "OIL CAN" BOYD, who, after being hos-
> pitalized for tests, labeled Boston Red Sox teammate
> Wade Boggs a "sex fiend"

Mental Muscle

Open up a ballplayer's head and you know what you'll find? A lot of
little broads and a jazz band.

> —MAYO SMITH, major league manager

The only qualifications for a lineman are to be big and dumb. To be a back, you only have to be dumb.

—KNUTE ROCKNE

If their IQs were five points lower they'd be geraniums.

—RUSS FRANCIS, New England Patriots tight end, assessing defensive linemen

I watched a lot of baseball on radio.

—GERALD FORD, former president

The trouble with [him] is that he played too many years without a helmet.

—LYNDON JOHNSON, observing a fellow onetime president, former University of Michigan center Gerald Ford

No, but they gave one to me anyway.

—ELDEN CAMPBELL, when the Los Angeles Lakers rookie was asked if he earned his degree at Clemson University

All a ballplayer has to do to be considered intellectual is read Kurt Vonnegut or own a Billy Joel album.

—FRANZ LIDZ, writer

Ninety percent of the game is half mental.

> —YOGI BERRA, on baseball, the thinking man's game

The good Lord was good to me. He gave me a strong body, a good right arm, and a weak mind.

> —DIZZY DEAN, Hall of Fame pitcher

What do you expect when they build a ball park on the ocean?

> —DENNIS "OIL CAN" BOYD, Boston Red Sox pitcher, commenting on the meteorologic conditions that can fog the brain—as well as Cleveland Stadium

A forty-million dollar airport—with a thirty-million dollar control tower.

> —RICK MONDAY, Los Angeles Dodgers outfielder, on San Francisco Giant Mike Ivie

Most Valuable Player from the neck down.

> —EDDIE STANKY, Chicago White Sox manager, suggesting Carl Yastrzemski's strong points during the American League's classic 1967 pennant race

On the White Sox' next visit to Boston, Fenway Park fans greeted Stanky with a huge banner proclaiming him "A Great Manager—From the Ankles Down." And refusing to be rattled, Yaz went on to capture the Triple Crown.

Don't read, it'll hurt your eyes.

> —SHOELESS JOE JACKSON, Chicago White Sox hitting star, before he was banished from baseball in the "Black Sox" scandal

The definition of a smart player is someone who can't play.

> —CAL McLISH, pitcher turned scout

Mind-Altering Substances

The way the Chargers played, the drug must have been formaldehyde.

> —BILL KURTIS, announcer, on allegations of drug abuse by the San Diego Chargers, 1966–77

Mistrust

Never trust a baserunner who's limping. Comes a base hit and you'll think he just got back from Lourdes.

> —JOE GARAGIOLA, catcher turned broadcaster

Money

You say to the youth of America, "Here is the opportunity," and the youth of America says, "How much are you going to pay me?"

> —CASEY STENGEL

Why should a guy with a half-million-dollar contract want to have blood dripping down his face? Or sweat? Or play with bruises? Hell, they won't even play with bruised feelings now.

> —BOBBY HULL, Hockey Hall of Famer and father of superstar Brett Hull

A ball player's got to be kept hungry to become a big leaguer. That's why no boy from a rich family ever made the big leagues.

> —JOE DiMAGGIO

The baseball player of today won't be satisfied until he plays two weeks in the big leagues and is able to retire at 22.

> —JOE GARAGIOLA, catcher turned broadcaster

Give him a couple of million. He shouldn't have to take a second job to support himself or anything.

> —JOSÉ CANSECO, Oakland A's slugger, explaining why Cincinnati Reds pitcher Ron Dibble should earn more than $200,000 a year

When you're playing for money, winning is the only thing that matters.

> —LEO DUROCHER

If you're paid before you walk on the court, what's the point in playing as if your life depended on it? Hell, if you've locked up a bundle of money from a challenge match, you might as well take a vacation the rest of the year.

> —ARTHUR ASHE, tennis pro, who opposed competitions that awarded players prearranged sums of money, regardless of who won

Everybody's negotiable.

> —MUHAMMAD ALI

A black man has to fight for respect in basketball, season after season. And I measure that respect in the figures on my contract.

> —KAREEM ABDUL-JABBAR

I had a better year than he did.

> —BABE RUTH, explaining why his $80,000 pay bid—$5,000 more than President Herbert Hoover's salary—was not unreasonable

Yankees owner Jake Ruppert apparently agreed. The Babe got the 80 thou.

Hit him with your wallet!

> —A Yankees teammate's advice to Roger Maris, who sometimes reportedly ended altercations with fans by taunting, "Oh, yeah? And how much money are you making?"

Whoever stole it is spending less than my wife.

> —ILIE NASTASE, tennis pro, commenting on his lost credit card

My money is my money.

> —PETE ROSE explaining why, though he was earning millions, his first wife shopped for clothes at K-Mart

Three years ago, Valenzuela's alarm clock was a rooster.

> —TOMMY LASORDA, Los Angeles Dodgers manager, on his ace pitcher's 1-million-dollar salary

Get your scorecard—names and numbers of all the millionaires.

> —Vendor at Shea Stadium

Nobody in football is worth a million dollars.

> —JOE PATERNO, Penn State football coach

The real superstar is a man or woman raising six kids on a hundred fifty dollars a week.

> —SPENCER HAYWOOD, basketball veteran

The Most Dangerous Game of All

Sex is a cure-all.

> —JOE NAMATH

Being with a woman all night never hurt no professional baseball player. It's staying up all night looking for a woman that does him in.

　　　　　—CASEY STENGEL

We prefer *wham, bam, thank-you-ma'am* affairs. In fact, if we're spotted taking a girl out to dinner we're accused of "wining and dining," which is bad form.

　　　　　—JIM BOUTON, pitcher turned author

I only go out with girls when I'm horny.

　　　　　—MARK "THE BIRD" FIDRYCH, pitcher

The only time sex has bothered me is when I do it during the competition.

　　　　　—BRUCE JENNER, Olympic decathlon champion

I certainly hope so.

　　　　　—KATE SCHMIDT, American javelin thrower, when
　　　　　　　asked if there had been any "fooling around" in
　　　　　　　the Olympic Village

Any girl who doesn't want to fuck can leave now.

　　　　　—BABE RUTH, at a 1928 party

I would still rather score a touchdown than make love to the prettiest girl in the United States.

> —PAUL HORNUNG, the Green Bay Packers bachelor, who had a reputation for scoring on and off the field

Mothers

You were great, Anthony, but your teammates stunk.

> —MONITA CARTER, after watching the Minnesota Vikings lose to the Dolphins despite four catches by her son

I have three sons. Which one do you mean?

> —ARVA ORR, Bobby's mother, when people asked "How's your son?"—obviously meaning the Boston Bruins superstar

Oh, the poor kid. He's going to get an ulcer now.

> —LAURA QUILICI, upon hearing that her son Frank had been named manager of the Minnesota Twins

I can't understand how she can ski down a mountain at 50 or 60 miles an hour, then come home and fall down the stairs.

> —HEATHER PERCY, mother of Canadian Olympic downhill skier Karen Percy

It's a good thing Brian was a third child, or he would have been the only one.

> —KATHY BOSWORTH, on her football-playing son, The Boz

What makes you think you're smarter than your daddy was?

> —Bill Veeck's mother, Grace, querying her son when he hired a new St. Louis Browns manager named Rogers Hornsby—the same choleric Hall of Famer that Veeck's father had fired as Chicago Cubs manager 20 years earlier

When Hornsby was canned after just two months, Momma Veeck wired Junior: "What did I tell you?"

Never take shit from nobody.

> —JENNY DOWNEY, dispensing motherly advice to her son Billy Martin.

"Mom never took shit from nobody," Billy said, recalling his four-foot-eleven mother in an autobiography. "It was her motto, something her mother taught her."

Mother's Mothers

That S.O.B.! If he hurt you I'll put a hex on him that he should never pitch again. His arms should fall off!

> —Mike Pagliarulo's grandmother, consoling the swollen-faced New York Yankees third baseman after a pitch broke his nose during a game at Oakland

Edwin doesn't have to fly that airplane. He just has to sit in it.

> —Duke Snider's grandmother, during a 1947 farewell
> party for the rookie outfielder as he headed for
> Dodger spring training, responding to the question
> "Don't you think Duke's having too many beers
> for someone flying to Cuba tonight?"

Dear Son:

Received your letter and am sorry to hear that you are so homesick.

You will notice that I did not forward any money for your passage to Philadelphia. The reason was not that I didn't have it to send to you, but that you were trying to tell me in your letter that you wanted to come home right away.

Edward, I have tears in my eyes while I'm telling this to you, but if you do come home, please do not come to 915 East Russell Street. We do not want quitters in this family.

Your Mother

> —Mother's letter to Eddie Stanky at the start of his
> professional baseball career—before he spent 17
> major league seasons as a feisty second base-
> man and manager with a hard-bitten
> reputation

The National Anthem

Once the national anthem plays, I get chills. I even know the words to it now.

—PETE ROSE

NBA Playoffs

They go on and on. It's like a guy telling a bad joke for 15 minutes.

—TOM HEINSOHN, Boston Celtics player, coach, and broadcaster

Negotiations

I signed Oscar Gamble on the advice of my attorney. I no longer have Gamble and I no longer have my attorney.

—RAY KROC, San Diego Padres owner

I got a million-dollars worth of free advice and a very small raise.

—EDDIE STANKY, Brooklyn Dodgers veteran, after negotiating his contract with boss Branch Rickey

They made me an offer I *could* refuse.

—ROD LAVER, rejecting a World Team Tennis bid

New York Yankees

From my experience, I've found that most organized crime figures are Yankees fans.

> —RICK MORANIS, in *My Blue Heaven*

[It] held all the carefree charm of a dentist's office.

> —JACK MANN, journalist, describing the sense of carefree camaraderie that permeated the Yankee clubhouse

When the Yankees go out for dinner, they reserve 25 tables for one.

> —An anonymous Yankees watcher

The Yankees ... are a family. A family like the Macbeths, the Borgias, and the Bordens of Fall River, Massachusetts.

> —RON FIMRITE, sportswriter

The myth is that you put a Yankee uniform on a player and he becomes great.

> —GEORGE "BIRDIE" TEBBETTS, former major league player, manager, general manager, and lifetime Yankees watcher

Hating the Yankees is as American as pizza pie, unwed mothers, and cheating on your income tax.

> —MIKE ROYKO, columnist

Rooting for the Yankees is like rooting for U.S. Steel.

> —RED SMITH, columnist, in 1951

I imagine rooting for the Yankees is like owning a yacht.

> —JIMMY CANNON, columnist

If you want to get off this team, you have to take a number.

> —DAVE REVERING, a veteran whose number came up shortly after he issued this statement

I want out. I'm sick of everything that goes on around here. I'm sick of all the negative stuff and you can take that upstairs to the fat man and tell him I said it.

> —GOOSE GOSSAGE, announcing that he is a pitcher beyond relief in 1982

When I was a kid, I wanted to play baseball and join the circus. With the Yankees I've been able to do both.

> —GRAIG NETTLES, who did both as captain

Nice Guys

Nice guys finish last.

> —LEO DUROCHER, Brooklyn Dodgers manager, on Mel Ott, New York Giants manager early in 1948 season

Not-so-nice-guy Durocher soon replaced nice-guy Ott that season and led the Giants to their legendary 1951 pennant.

Nicknames

I refuse to call a 52-year-old man "Sparky."

> —AL CLARK, umpire, explaining why he addressed
> the Detroit Tigers manager as *George* Anderson

The Boston Strangler.

> —KEVIN PAUL DUPONT, sportswriter, nicknaming
> Brad McCrimmon in the *Boston Globe* after the
> Detroit Red Wings defenseman allegedly choked
> Boston Bruins wing Jeff Lazaro while the two
> were buried beneath a pileup during a game-ending
> melee at Boston Garden

Long after the ice was cleared, two physicians worked to restore the breathing of the prostrate Lazaro, who later claimed, "I was fighting for my life."

McCrimmon received no extra punishment beyond what some fellow brawlers got. Television cameras could not capture the activity beneath the pileup. Besides, as Bruins assistant coach Mike O'Connell puckishly noted, "There's nothing in the rule book about strangulation, is there?"

No Bull

I didn't try too hard. I was afraid I'd get emotionally involved with the cow.

> —ROCKY BRIDGES, minor league manager,
> after competing in a pregame milking
> contest

No Mercy

I don't care if he has no feet.

> —TY COBB, after vaulting into a grandstand in 1912
> and stomping an abusive heckler, only to learn
> that the heckler had no hands.

For the record, Cobb's tormentor actually had two fingers, having lost one hand and three fingers in a printing accident a year earlier. It is not clear from the reports whether the loudmouth was giving Cobb the finger with one of his remaining fingers. In any case, Cobb won, hands down.

Not-So-Gracious Winners

What are they going to do with all of those [blankety-blank] balloons now? Anybody want to buy some balloons cheap?

> —ARNOLD "RED" AUERBACH, Boston
> Celtics guru, as he danced gleefully across the
> Los Angeles Forum basketball court after his

1969 Celtics clinched another NBA championship, laughing and pointing to the rafters, where
nets held countless balloons in anticipation of
a Lakers victory that didn't happen

Nun Sense

Get in there and kick some ass. God be with you.

—A Massachusetts nun wiring advice and inspiration
to hard-luck Boston reliever Bob Stanley after
the Red Sox' gut-wrenching, one-strike-away loss
to the New York Mets in game six of the
1986 World Series

Officiating, Boomerang

Decisions of the judges will be final unless shouted down by a really
overwhelming majority of the crowd present.

—Rules of the first open boomerang tournament at
Washington, D.C., in 1974

On the Road

"Two Rogers? You mean there'll be one home now?"

—KATHY PENSKE, wife of veteran Indy-car
racer Roger Penske, upon learning that a
life-size statue of her husband had just been
commissioned

Orders

Bonehead, get up there and bat!

>   —GEORGE STALLINGS, manager of the
>   1914 "Miracle Braves," whereupon
>   seven bench-warmers leaped for the bat
>   rack

Orders from on High

There will be no more acts of God.

>   —KENESAW MOUNTAIN LANDIS, baseball's
>   no-nonsense first commissioner, warning
>   Bill Veeck that there must be no repeats of
>   his Milwaukee club's arc-light failure,
>   which occurred, coincidentally, just as the
>   home-team Brewers were on the brink of
>   losing their lead. Veeck, who operated the
>   then minor-league Brewers, had termed
>   the occurrence "an act of God."

"Out" on Tour

LPGA: Lesbian Professional Golf Association.

>   —Unattributed acronym quoted in the *New York Times*

Owners

A fellow bossing a big league ball club is busier than a one-armed paperhanger with the flying hives.

> —TY COBB, who managed as well as starred for the Detroit Tigers

As men get older, their toys get more expensive.

> —MARVIN DAVIS, who thought he had purchased the Oakland A's for more than $12 million—a deal that would unravel

Owners on Owners

He's the kind of a guy Dale Carnegie would punch in the mouth.

> —BILL VEECK, on fellow owner Walter O'Malley

Turner must be insane. This must be insanity.

> —EDWARD BENNETT WILLIAMS, Baltimore Orioles owner, on Ted Turner after hearing that the Atlanta Braves owner had paid $3½ million for journeyman Claudell Washington

Dislike? Hell, I hate the son of a bitch!

> —GENE KLEIN, San Diego Chargers owner, when asked during a deposition if he "disliked" Oakland Raiders boss Al Davis

He's an asshole.... If you don't put a guy like Davis in his place, pretty soon you got no league left.

—GENE KLEIN on Al Davis—again

Most people know Barron doesn't have an overabundance of brains. The smartest thing he ever did was pick his father.

—GENE KLEIN, during a feud with San Diego Chargers partner Barron Hilton, Conrad's son

Owners Put Down by Players

That son of a bitch is goofier than both of us.

—JIMMY PIERSALL, former sanatorium resident, to mule "Charlie O" while observing Oakland A's owner Charles O. Finley raving and ranting during the 1972 World Series

When Charlie had his heart operation, it took eight hours—seven and a half just to find his heart.

—STEVE McCATTY, Oakland A's pitcher, on Charles O. Finley

If you didn't have any tickets to give away, you wouldn't have any friends.

—JOHN MACKEY, Football/Hall of Famer, to Baltimore Colts owner Carroll Rosenbloom

When I played, the players were dumb. Now the owners are.

> —MICKEY MANTLE, slugger who never earned more than $100,000 a season, commenting on today's instant-multimillionaire baseball salaries

Parental Advice

Oh, Butch, you're not going to have to go to that animal farm, are you?

> —Butch Wynegar's mother on hearing that her son had been traded to the Yankees

Philanthropy

And now the pretty little girls will press among you with their little cans. Please give until it hurts!

> —HARRY BALOGH, public address announcer at the old Madison Square Garden, makes a plea for the March of Dimes

Physical Fitness

As a nation we are dedicated to keeping physically fit—and parking as close to the stadium as possible.

> —BILL VAUGHN, writer

The worst of this is that I can no longer see my penis when I stand up.

> —BABE RUTH, on the downside of his bulging belly

I don't know. I'm not in shape yet.

> —YOGI BERRA, when asked to estimate his cap size

I get my exercise acting as pallbearer to my friends who exercise.

> —CHAUNCEY DEPEW, attorney and wit

If running was so important, Jesse Owens would be a twenty-game winner.

> —ART FOWLER, pitcher and pitching coach

All that running and exercise can do for you is make you healthy.

> —DENNY McLAIN, two-time Cy Young Award winner

Whenever I feel like exercise, I lie down until the feeling passes.

> —ROBERT HUTCHINS, educator

I won't say I'm out of condition now, but I even puff going downstairs.

> —DICK GREGORY, comic and activist

A really fat man is no good at the game of golf because if he tees the ball where he can hit it, he can't see it; and if he puts the ball where he can see it, he can't hit it.

> —ANONYMOUS

You're never too old to do what you want if you're fat enough.

> —GEORGE FOREMAN, heavyweight champion—and truly a *heavy*weight

Pitchers

I said, "Moe, look around you. Where the fuck are you going to put him?"

> —FRED HUTCHINSON, Cincinnati Reds manager, recalling what he said to pitcher Moe Drabowsky during a ninth-inning, bases-loaded trip to the mound

What do they want me to do? Let them sons of bitches stand up there and think on my time?

> —GROVER CLEVELAND ALEXANDER, 373-game winner, on why he wasted no time between pitches

Why should I worry about batters? Do they worry about me? Do you ever find a hitter crying because he's hit a line drive through the box? My job is getting hitters out. If I don't get them out, I lose. I've got a right to knock down anybody holding a bat.

> —EARLY WYNN, 300-game winner

Most pitchers are too smart to manage.

> —JIM PALMER, three-time Cy Young Award winner

Poets are like baseball pitchers. Both have their moments. The intervals are the tough things.

>—ROBERT FROST, a poet who knew his baseball

It's a shame the young Met pitchers aren't on a big league team.

>—JIMMY CANNON, columnist

Players' Revenge

He's a cold man, with no human understanding in him.

>—DON MEREDITH, quarterback turned broad-
>caster, on his former Dallas Cowboys coach, Tom
>Landry

Pleas

Say it ain't so, Joe. Say it ain't so.

>—A small boy clutching the arm of Shoeless Joe
>Jackson as the "Black Sox" star departed the
>Chicago Grand Jury inquiry into the fixing of
>the 1919 World Series

"Yes, kid, I'm afraid it is," Jackson was quoted as answering in the next day's Chicago Herald *and* Examiner. *"Well," said the lad, "I never would've thought it."*

Poetic License to Kill

Mother, may I slug the umpire?
May I slug him right away?
So he cannot be here, mother,
When the clubs begin to play?

Let me clasp his throat, dear mother,
In a dear, delightful grip,
With one hand and with the other
Bat him several on the lip.

Let me climb his frame, dear mother,
While the happy people shout,
I'll not kill him, dearest mother,
I will only knock him out.

Let me mop the ground up, mother,
With his person, dearest do,
If the ground can stand it, mother,
I don't see why you can't, too.

> —Anonymous irate fan, c. 1886

Baseball followers were then known as "cranks"—for obvious reasons.

Post This

I would rather have my kids find a *Hustler* magazine around the house than a *New York Post*.... At least the *National Enquirer* admits that it makes up some of its stories.

> —GRAIG NETTLES, Yankees third baseman and
> captain

Pray for Money

We're going to get the best women's basketball team money can buy...within the rules, of course.

—REV. ORAL ROBERTS, on his university's plans

Prejudice

I ain't got no quarrel with them Vietcong. They never called me "nigger."

—MUHAMMAD ALI, who refused military induction in 1966 on the grounds that he was a conscientious objector

Prejudice in Sports

Get that nigger off the field!

—ADRIAN "POP" ANSON, star first baseman–manager of the Chicago White Stockings and noted racist, bellowing in protest when he saw Moses "Fleetwood" Walker, a black catcher, on the diamond for Toledo before a game with Chicago

Anson was one of the greatest players in early baseball, and he used his power to keep blacks out of organized baseball—a literal blacklisting that lasted until after World War II.

This must be a big event for Atlanta. I hear the Regency Hotel is full up with colored people.

> —MUHAMMAD ALI, before his triumphant return to boxing in 1970 against Jerry Quarry

Ali scored a third-round knockout, ending his nearly 3½-year exile from boxing.

You'd be amazed at the places segregation pops up in. I went out to the racetrack last week—every horse I bet on was shuffled to the rear.

> —DICK GREGORY, comic and activist

Christ-killer!

> —Chicago Cubs bench jockeys taunting Jewish umpire Dolly Stark during the 1935 World Series

In the same series, the Cubs also "crucified Hank Greenberg [the Detroit Tigers star] for being a Jew," according to George Moriarty, who also umpired that series.

But I'm only half Jewish. Can't I play nine holes?

> —BARRY GOLDWATER, politician, when told he could not play at a private golf club

I'll integrate my team when Abe Saperstein integrates his.

> —GEORGE PRESTON MARSHALL, owner of the Washington Redskins, the last NFL team to integrate, referring to the founder and operator of the all-black Harlem Globetrotters

Golf...I get it. A couple of blond Nazis walking through the woods with two spades carrying their shit.

> —DAN JENKINS, novelist and humorist, defining the game

I don't give a damn if he's striped or polka dot or plaid. Boston takes Charles Cooper of Duquesne.

> —WALTER BROWN, Celtics owner, repeating Boston's 1950 selection of the first black player ever chosen in the NBA draft, after a fellow owner broke the meeting's stunned silence with "Walter, don't you know he's a colored boy?"

The basketball is a tool that the black has now, same as maybe he once had a plow.

> —WILLIS REED, Basketball Hall of Famer

The worst prejudice in sports isn't skin color, it is size.

> —CALVIN MURPHY, five-nine guard for the Houston Rockets

I have always said it's more important who's going to be the first black sports editor of the *New York Times* than the first black baseball manager.

—BILL RUSSELL, Basketball Hall of Famer and the NBA's first black coach

Baseball is very big with my people. It figures. It's the only time we can get to shake a stick at a white man without starting a riot.

—DICK GREGORY, comic and activist

Before that black son of a bitch accuses us of being prejudiced, he should learn how to hit an Indian.

—CASEY STENGEL on Jackie Robinson, after the Brooklyn Dodgers star was fanned three times by New York Yankees pitcher Allie Reynolds, part Cree

The reason baseball has no black managers or general managers is that I truly believe that they may not have some of the necessities to be, let's say, a field manager.

Why are black men, or black people, not good swimmers? Because they don't have the buoyancy.

—AL CAMPANIS, soon-to-be former Los Angeles Dodgers general manager, to Ted Koppel on ABC-TV's "Nightline," in April 1987

In 1944, before he died . . . [Commissioner] Landis said, "Everything has been said that's going to be said. The answer is no." He was adamant. If you had black skin, that automatically disqualified you from the majors. . . .

For 24 years, Judge Landis . . . had not let blacks into the majors. Suppose Landis had been commissioner in 1947 and Rickey had asked Landis to approve the transfer, what do you think Landis would have said?

> —A. B. "HAPPY" CHANDLER, Landis' successor, approving Branch Rickey's 1947 request to transfer Jackie Robinson's contract from the Brooklyn Dodgers' Montreal affiliate to the parent club despite the baseball owners' reported 15–1 mandate against breaking the major leagues' race barrier

I'm not going to play with any nigger. I think I'll go home and paint my house.

> —FRED "DIXIE" WALKER, Brooklyn Dodgers outfielder, when Jackie Robinson joined the team in 1947, integrating major league baseball

I don't care if the guy is yellow or black or if he has stripes like a fuckin' zebra. I'm the manager of this team and I say he plays.

> —LEO DUROCHER, telling his 1947 Brooklyn Dodgers in spring training that Jackie Robinson would play despite some team grumbling

Why should I read about a man playing a game that I couldn't get into at the time?

> —HENRY AARON, explaining why he knew so little about Babe Ruth, the slugging legend he succeeded as baseball's all-time home run leader

If a Latin player is sick, they say it is all in his mind.

> —ROBERTO CLEMENTE, reacting to suggestions that he was a malingerer

You ignorant, ill-bred foreigners! If you don't like the way I'm doing things out there, why don't you just pack up and go back to your own countries!

> —CHIEF BENDER, early-century Native American pitcher, to booing fans

Profanity

I'll always remember Tom Heinsohn's pep talks. One time there were 72 bleeps in it—and that was Christmas Day.

> —PAUL WESTPHAL, Boston Celtics forward

George Shaw would make a good quarterback if he could just learn to say "shit."

> —ALLIE SHERMAN, New York Giants coach, on his unprofane quarterback

All pro athletes are bilingual. They speak English and profanity.

> —GORDIE HOWE, Hockey Hall of Famer

Professional Sports

Professional sports should be reported on the entertainment pages along with circuses and vaudeville.

> —AVERY BRUNDAGE, longtime Olympic czar

Professionalism

"How you play the game" is for college boys. When you're playing for money, winning is the only thing that matters.

> —LEO DUROCHER, shortstop, manager, and pool shark

Psyching Your Team

I think we can win it—if my brains hold out.

> —JOHN McGRAW, manager, during the
> 1921 pennant race (his brains did—and
> his New York Giants did)

Pump Me Up

Many times at the beach a good-looking lady will say to me, "I want to touch you." I always smile and say, "I don't blame you."

> —ARNOLD SCHWARZENEGGER, six-time
> "Mr. Universe"

Putdowns of Spectators Sitting Next to You

That so? Which team were you playing on?

> —JOHN BARRYMORE, actor, when a boor boasted,
> "When I was in college, I helped Harvard beat
> Yale three times in succession"

Put Them All Together, They Spell...Beanball

Even if my mom stands up at the plate and I have to knock her down, I'll do it. That's my job.

> —PASCUAL PÉREZ, New York Yankees pitcher, on
> Mother's Day, 1991

Quote Even We Can't Believe

She could have urinated on him.

> —DON KING, fight promoter, telling talk-show king
> Larry King how easily Desiree Washington could
> have prevented Mike Tyson from performing oral
> sex on her in an Indianapolis hotel room

Quotes on Quotes

I really didn't say everything I said.

> —YOGI BERRA

I hate quotations.

> —RALPH WALDO EMERSON

Recruiting

One of these days the NCAA might put in a rule that says you have to have one player on your team from your home state.

> —ABE LEMONS, University of Texas
> basketball coach

Religion

God is always on the side that has the best football coach.

> —HEYWOOD HALE BROUN, columnist

God is on our side.

> —DON KING, fight promoter, explaining why Mike
> Tyson's rape and deviate sexual conduct convictions
> would be overturned on appeal

An atheist is a guy who watches a Notre Dame—SMU football game and doesn't care who wins.

> —DWIGHT EISENHOWER, a president who knew
> his way around a gridiron from his days as a West
> Point football player

Leisure is the handmaiden of the devil.

> —BRANCH RICKEY, baseball executive who didn't
> attend games on Sunday, his sabbath

He might have found Jesus, but he's having a terrible time finding [Haven] Moses.

> —MORRIS SIEGEL, columnist, critiquing the Super
> Bowl XII passing performance of born-again Chris-
> tian Craig Morton

JESUS SAVES—And Espo Scores on the Rebound!

> —Boston bumper sticker heralding the scoring prowess
> of Phil Esposito during the seventies heyday of the
> "Big, Bad Bruins"

The Lord taught me to love everybody, but the last ones I learned to love were the sportswriters.

> —ALVIN DARK, Oakland A's manager

Let's get rid of these guys and get new ones. That's what the Lord did. He drowned them all and started over with two of each kind.

> —TED TURNER, Atlanta Braves owner, on the theology
> of trades—during his team's laughingstock days, before
> it won a dramatic pennant and captured the nation's
> fancy

If Jesus Christ were to show up with his old baseball glove, some guys wouldn't vote for him. He dropped the cross three times, didn't he?

—DICK YOUNG, columnist, writing why Willie Mays wasn't unanimously voted into the Hall of Fame

God speaks to me, too, and He hasn't told me to help you.

—JESSE BARFIELD, responding to born-again fans who ask him for money

Please God, let me hit one. I'll tell everybody You did it.

—REGGIE JACKSON, in prayer

If God let you hit a home run last time up, then who struck you out the time before that?

—SPARKY ANDERSON, manager

KNICKS CUT CHRIST

—Headline when the New York Knickerbockers waived Fred Christ in 1954 after the rookie from Fordham averaged 3.3 points in six NBA games

Respect for Literature

Fuck you, Shakespeare!

—PETE ROSE, yelling out to the mound to Jim Bouton, referring to the pitcher's winning ways with written words

We're coming at you, Keats!

> —JOHNNY UNITAS, quarterback, hollering across scrimmage to defensive back Daryl Johnson, who had been rhyming poetically in Boston newspapers about how the Patriots would defeat the Baltimore Colts

Rodeo

Rodeoing is about the only sport you can't fix. You'd have to talk to the bulls and horses, and they wouldn't understand you.

> —BILL LUNDERMAN, rodeo champion

Spinning a rope's a lot of fun—providing your neck ain't in it.

> —WILL ROGERS

Rubbing It In

The only time Jimmy didn't run up a score was 27 years ago when he took the SAT.

> —JIM NANTZ, sportscaster, on football coach Jimmy Johnson

Rugby

I prefer rugby to soccer. When soccer players start biting each other's ears off, maybe I'll like it better.

> —ELIZABETH TAYLOR, actress

Sailing

The fine art of getting wet and becoming ill while slowly going nowhere at great expense.

> —HENRY BEARD and ROY McKIE, authors, defining the sport

The Scouting Report

Good field, no hit.

> —MIGUEL "MIKE" GONZALEZ, Cuban-born catcher, coach, and scout, sizing up a twenties prospect with a terse appraisal that has become a part of baseball's lexicon

G'wan, get outa here. Go get a shoebox.

> —CASEY STENGEL, Brooklyn Dodgers manager, shooing away a scrawny teenager named Phil Rizzuto during a tryout for sandlotters in the thirties

Rizzuto would later become Stengel's star shortstop during a New York Yankees' dynasty—before Casey again cut him during the 1956 season.

Champion of the world, my eye. That kid ain't got the guts to fill a thimble.

> —JERRY LISKER, sportswriter, appraising young Cassius Clay, before he became Muhammad Ali

The kid will never last more than two or three years.

> —GINO MARCHETTI, Baltimore Colts defensive end, predicting the future of a scrambling quarterback named Fran Tarkenton

Second Guessing

Second guessing *is* sports.

> —MIKE LUPICA, columnist

Self-Promotion

Some folks leave their brains to science. But when I go, I'm leaving my mouth. It's the greatest!

> —CASSIUS CLAY, before he changed his name if not his tune

Sex vs. Sports

Unless there's an emotional tie, I'd rather play tennis.

> —BIANCA JAGGER, the former Mrs. Mick, on the importance of sex

She's Gone Too Far

I've taken this team as far as I can.

> —LYNN WHEELER, upon resigning as coach of the
> Iowa State women's basketball team after 14
> consecutive losses

Signs

JUMP, ART!

> —Sign in Cleveland Stadium directed at Browns owner
> Art Modell, which was quickly confiscated by sta-
> dium security

YOU CAN'T TOUCH THIS, ART!

> —Banner trailed by a circling airplane during the Browns'
> next home game

Size

Bambi, America's favorite midget.

> —JIM McMAHON, in a frequent reference to fellow
> quarterback and onetime Chicago Bears teammate
> Doug Flutie

No, I clean giraffe ears.

> —ELVIN HAYES, six-foot-nine NBA star, when asked
> one time too many if he played basketball

I thought maybe we should have hit him [with the pitch]. But I didn't want to face a homicide charge.

> —BOB SWIFT, Detroit Tigers catcher, that memorable
> 1951 afternoon when three-foot-seven, 65-pound
> Eddie Gaedel, wearing number ⅛, pinch-hit for the
> St. Louis Browns

The bigger they are, the harder they fall.

> —BOB FITZSIMMONS, 167-pound heavyweight
> champ, taunting 205-pound challenger Jim Jeffries
> before their 1899 title fight

It was Fitzsimmons who ultimately fell, knocked out in the 11th round—and proving it was no fluke, he was KO'd a second time in a rematch.

Six Feet under Par

We believe that golfers have a more personal attachment for their golf clubs [courses] and its members than for an anonymous space in a public cemetery.

> —Mod-Urn Columbarium Gardens
> representative explaining a plan to
> bury up to 2,000 golfers on courses
> around the world

Slumps

I'm playing like Tarzan—and scoring like Jane.

> —CHI CHI RODRIGUEZ, pro golfer

When you are in a slump and you have all that stuff in your mind, medically speaking, you need a mental enema.

> —FRAN HEALY, catcher turned announcer

My bats are in Mexico, undergoing laetrile treatments.

> —MARTY CASTILLO, Detroit Tigers utility man

The only people in the U.S. who had a worse night than me died.

> —STEVE KEMP, veteran outfielder after a forgettable game

Soccer

A guy scores a goal, runs around the stadium shaking his fists, suddenly sinks to his knees, and everybody on the team fucks him dog-style.

> —DAN JENKINS, defining the sport

Sour Grapes: The Breakfast of Champions

I'm going to knock the next pitch down your goddamned throat.

> —What Babe Ruth allegedly *really* said to Chicago Cubs
> pitcher Charlie Root when The Bambino "called

> his shot" into Wrigley Field's center field bleachers
> during the 1932 World Series

Yogi is a completely manufactured product. He is a case study of this country's unlimited ability to gull itself and be gulled.

> —BILL VEECK, who knew something about gulling
> himself as baseball's master showman

Spitballers

He talks very well for a guy who's had two fingers in his mouth all his life.

> —GENE MAUCH, who scrutinized opposing
> pitchers 35 years as player and manager,
> complimenting spitballer-turned-broadcaster
> Don Drysdale

Drysdale refuted the charge, saying, "My mother told me never to put my dirty fingers in my mouth."

I'll just hit the dry side of the ball.

> —STAN MUSIAL, Hall of Fame hitter, revealing how
> he planned to handle Preacher Roe's spitball

Reduce the load of juice, Gaylord. [Umpire Ed] Sudol's getting suspicious of that splashing sound in my mitt.

> —TOM HALLER, catcher, warning San Francisco Giants
> battery-mate Gaylord Perry, who moistened more than
> a few pitches en route to Cooperstown

300 Wins Is Nothing To Spit At.

>—GAYLORD PERRY's T-shirt inscription when he
>notched his 300th victory in 1982

Sport Shooting

A sportsman is a man who, every now and then, simply has to get out and kill something.

>—STEPHEN LEACOCK, author

The fascination of shooting as a sport depends almost wholly on whether you are at the right or wrong end of a gun.

>—P. G. WODEHOUSE, author

It depends on whom you kill.

>—GEORGE BERNARD SHAW, when asked by Lady
>Astor whether he hated killing for pleasure

Sports

Sports is the toy department of human life.

>—HOWARD COSELL, broadcaster

I hate all sports as rabidly as a person who likes sports hates common sense.

>—H. L. MENCKEN

Sports and Television

Unquestionably, TV is saving sports, although I'm not sure sports is worth saving.

—HOWARD COSELL, broadcaster

Sports as Therapy

I was in group analysis when I was younger. . . . I was the captain of the latent paranoid softball team. We used to play the neurotics on Sunday mornings. The nail biters against the bed wetters. If you've never seen neurotics play softball, it's pretty funny. I used to steal second base, then feel guilty and go back.

—WOODY ALLEN, moviemaker

Sportscasting

With few exceptions, sports broadcasters function as publicity men, not reporters.

—JIMMY CANNON, columnist

The Washington Senators and the New York Giants must have played a doubleheader this afternoon—the game I saw and the game Graham McNamee announced.

—RING LARDNER, writer, who sat next to McNamee as the sportscasting pioneer aired a 1924 World Series game, the first broadcast ever direct from a U.S. playing site

He announced a football game like a holdup victim hollering for a cop.

> —JIMMY CANNON, columnist, describing Harry Wismer's broadcasting style

I tell it like it is. Howard Cosell tells it like Roone Arledge wants it told.

> —HARRY CARAY, baseball broadcaster

Sportsmanship

Who is this guy, Queensberry? I don't see anything wrong in sticking your thumb into any guy's eye. Just a little.

> —"TWO-TON" TONY GALENTO, journeyman heavyweight, to a boxing commissioner

It's good sportsmanship to not pick up lost golf balls while they are still rolling.

> —MARK TWAIN

He was their best player. . . . I can't explain it . . . sometimes you get mad. . . . I get mad if I think someone is damaging my team.

> —CARLOS ALBERTO, New York Cosmo, trying to explain why he kicked Dallas Tornado star Omar Gomez, knocking him out of a 1980 soccer game the Cosmos proceeded to win

Show me a sportsman and I'll show you a player I'm looking to trade.

> —LEO DUROCHER

I hope he sinks.

—TED TURNER, on a yachting rival before the 1977 America's Cup

Sports Viewing

If we did get a divorce, the only way he would know it is if they announced it on "Wide World of Sports."

—DR. JOYCE BROTHERS, on her sports-addicted husband

Statistics

Statistics are about as interesting as first-base coaches.

—STEVE SAX, veteran second baseman

Statistics are like a girl in a fine bikini; it shows a lot but it doesn't show everything.

—TOBY HARRAH, veteran infielder

Statistics are used by baseball fans in much the same way that a drunk leans against a street lamp; it's there more for support than enlightenment.

—VIN SCULLY, announcer

I am quite sure that statistics will show that the greatest number of successes have been scored by those who have led moderately dirty lives.

—W. O. McGEEHAN, columnist

Steinbrenner, George

GIVE ME A BASTARD WITH TALENT.

—Message on a pillow in George Steinbrenner's office

I won't be active in the day-to-day operations of the club at all. I'll stick to ships.

—GEORGE STEINBRENNER, shortly after buying the New York Yankees in 1973

It's a beautiful thing to behold, with all 36 oars working in unison.

—JACK BUCK, announcer, on George Steinbrenner's newly acquired yacht

The more we lose, the more Steinbrenner will fly in. And the more he flies, the better the chance there will be a plane crash.

—Attributed to various Yankees

He really should stick to horses. At least he can shoot them if they spit the bit.

—REGGIE JACKSON

You measure the value of a ballplayer on how many fannies he puts in the seats.

> —GEORGE STEINBRENNER

Seeing how none of us ever worked for Genghis Khan, how does it feel to work for George Steinbrenner?

> —TED DAWSON, broadcaster, interviewing New York Yankees manager Gene Michael

George Steinbrenner talks out of both sides of his wallet.

> —RON LUCIANO, umpire turned author

I know how to tell when George Steinbrenner is lying. His lips move.

> —JERRY REINSDORF, Chicago White Sox co-owner

The Yankees owner labeled Reinsdorf and partner Eddie Einhorn "the Abbott and Costello of baseball . . . a pair of Katzenjammer Kids."

I've always said that if you wait and keep your mouth shut, things will come around right.

> —GEORGE STEINBRENNER

Steroids

We came here to swim, not sing.

> —Unidentified East German swimming coach,
> responding to a rival who noted that
> many of his female swimmers had unusually
> low voices—a telltale clue of anabolic
> steroid use

And Still Champion...

Fifty years old, 212 fights, and I'm still pretty.

> —MUHAMMAD ALI, then in a fight with Parkinson's
> syndrome, showing celebrants at his 50th birthday
> party in a Los Angeles theater that he's still the
> greatest

The Stuff from Which Enduring Memories Are Made

Even to this day, some people look at me like I'm a piece of shit.

> —JOHNNY PESKY, Boston Red Sox institution who,
> nearly a half-century later, is still haunted by an
> alleged pause on his relay as St. Louis Cardinal Enos
> Slaughter slid home with the deciding run of the
> 1946 World Series

Stupidity

At my stupidest, I was never as stupid as the Boston Red Sox.

> —TED TURNER, Atlanta Braves owner

Superbowl

If this was the ultimate game, they wouldn't be playing it again next year.

> —DUANE THOMAS, Dallas Cowboys rookie running-back sensation, during 1970 Superbowl week in Miami

Sweet Dreams

You gotta sleep before you can have nightmares.

> —ARMAND "BEP" GUIDOLIN, coach, when asked if his expansion Kansas City Scouts (now New Jersey Devils) gave him nightmares

Swimming (Sour Grapes Division)

It could have happened to a nicer guy.

> —DOUG RUSSELL, who beat Mark Spitz in the 100-meter butterfly at the 1968 Olympics in Mexico City, commenting on Spitz's seven gold medals in the 1972 games in Munich

Swimming, Unique Strategies in

Sure. I'd float across on the garbage.

> —GERTRUDE EDERLE, who prepared for her 1926 conquest of the English Channel by swimming 21 miles through New York Bay, when asked if she could do the same in 1973

Teams Are Really Just Like Families

They'd find room for Charles Manson if he could hit .300.

> —JIM BOUTON, pitcher turned author

Team Spirit

He's got a square jaw, and a square head, and both match his personality.

> —JOHNNY BENCH, describing longtime Cincinnati Reds teammate Pete Rose

He has the personality of a tree trunk.

> —JOHN STEARNS, catcher, on New York Mets teammate Dave Kingman

The only thing Reggie can do better than me on the field is talk.

> —ROD CAREW, on California Angels teammate Reggie Jackson

If I had a knife, I would have stabbed him.

> —DAN HAMPTON, after Chicago Bears teammate Brad Muster fumbled

I'm going to party. I got no reason not to.

> —DENNIS "OIL CAN" BOYD, the emotional Boston Red Sox right-hander, as he exited a New York hotel in tears after being told that, because of that day's rain postponement, he would not start game seven of the 1986 World Series the following night

I'd rather play in hell than for the Angels.

> —ALEX JOHNSON, who won a batting championship for the 1970 California Angels

This team finished last on merit.

> —BRANCH RICKEY, general manager, on his awful 1952 Pittsburgh Pirates

What we're trying to do here is make chicken salad out of chicken shit.

> —JOE KUHEL, manager, on his rock-bottom 1949 Washington Senators

We're the only team in history that could lose nine games in a row and then go into a slump.

> —BILL FITCH, coach, on his early Cleveland Cavaliers

I've never seen such stupid ballplaying in my life.

> —RAY KROC, San Diego Padres owner, seizing the public address microphone and apologizing to San Diego fans

We was going to get him a birthday cake, but we figured he'd drop it.

> —CASEY STENGEL, on New York Mets cult figure Marvelous Marv Throneberry

We were as flat as a plate of piss.

> —JOE SCHMIDT, coach, on his Detroit Lions' losing performance

Dissension? We got no dissension. What we ain't got is pitchers.

> —ROY CAMPANELLA, catcher, on the 1950 Brooklyn Dodgers

I don't think either team can win it.

> —WARREN BROWN, sportswriter, previewing what would be dubbed "The World's Worst Series" in 1945 between the Chicago Cubs and Detroit Tigers

Television

The best show on television is Red Sox baseball. Everything else sucks.

> —STEPHEN KING, novelist and Boston Red Sox addict from Maine

Tennis

How to shake hands.

> —BETTINA BUNGE, when asked what she learned from 11 consecutive losses to Martina Navratilova

I have to get mad to win.

> —CHRIS EVERT LLOYD, who needs only to read the following quote to get mad

Tennis—Advice

Hit at the girl whenever possible.

> —BILL TILDEN, amateur champion, on how to win at mixed doubles

Tennis Fans

There's a different breed of cats coming out here. Instead of hoi polloi, we're now getting the Johnny Six-Pack.

—MIKE BLANCHARD, Forest Hills
tournament referee, in 1977

Tennis, Predictability of

They ought to play the women's finals on opening day. Everybody knows who's going to be in it.

—JIMMY CONNORS, tennis pro

Tennis, Putting It in Perspective

You hear an announcer saying at a tennis match, "On this serve rests $40,000." Imagine saying that about a sonata performed by Serkin.

—HENRY STEELE COMMAGER, historian

Those Who Can't: Columnists, Journalists, and Other Sideliners

A [sports] journalist is someone who would if he could but he can't, so he tells those who already can how they should.

—CLIFF TEMPLE, British sportswriter

To hell with newspapermen. You can buy them with a steak.

> —GEORGE WEISS, New York Yankees general manager

Nothing on earth is more depressing than an old baseball writer.

> —RING LARDNER, an old baseball writer

If I ever need a brain transplant, I want one from a sportswriter because I'll know it's never been used.

> —JOE PATERNO, Penn State football coach

You've got to be an idiot.

> —ROGER MARIS, New York Yankees slugger, in response to a reporter who asked, during Maris' 61-homer summer of '61, what a .260 hitter was doing hitting all those home runs

No, journalism. It was easier.

> —JOE NAMATH, quarterback, when asked if he had studied basket weaving at the University of Alabama

Most guys who write about sports are just little overweight creeps.

> —PETE MARAVICH, who always appeared underweight as a basketball star

The big thing is that the writers are not around demoralizing the players.

> —DENNY McLAIN, pitcher, giving a Detroit newspaper strike credit for helping the Tigers' drive to the 1968 World Championship

Only when I look at you.

> —JIM McMAHON, quarterback, when asked by a reporter if he was in pain

I go to the park sick as a dog, and when I see my uniform hanging there I get well right now. Then I see some of you guys and I get sick again.

> —PETE ROSE, greeting the press

Absolute silence—that's the one thing a sportswriter can quote accurately.

> —BOBBY KNIGHT, Indiana basketball coach

I have nothing to say to a bunch of whores.

> —LAWRENCE TAYLOR, New York Giants linebacker, to a gaggle of reporters inquiring about his marital difficulties

I'm in room 123. Go up and write a column and a sidebar.

> —WOODY PAIGE, sportswriter, responding to a woman in a hotel bar who assured him she'd do anything he wanted for $100

Here's a dime. Call all your friends.

> —TOM MEANY, to a critical fellow sportswriter

I'll bet more people have gone to sleep reading newspapers than watching ball games.

> —CHARLIE MAXWELL, Detroit Tigers outfielder, responding to a sportswriter who said he needed something to keep him awake while watching the Tigers

Ya see, I said "fuck" to ruin his audio. Then when I started scratching my ass I ruined his video. He ain't gonna ask me a question like that again.

> —CASEY STENGEL, explaining his f-word response to a reporter who asked whether his New York Yankees choked in the 1957 World Series

It's like listening to New York Yankees announcer Phil Rizzuto during a rain delay.

> —DAVID LETTERMAN, explaining what it's like being dead

When they circumcised him they threw away the wrong part.

> —GEORGE PRESTON MARSHALL, Washington Redskins owner, on a Washington sports columnist

Pour hot water over a sportswriter and you get instant horseshit.

—TED WILLIAMS

Threats

If you guys don't shut up, I'll put on my old Yankee uniform and scare you to death.

—WAITE HOYT, Pittsburgh Pirates pitcher and New York Yankees alumnus, to a dugout of jeering Chicago Cubs, a team humbled in the 1932 World Series, four games to none, by his former Bronx Bomber mates

Tieing

A tie is like kissing your sister.

—DUFFY DAUGHERTY, Michigan State football coach

Everybody says a tie is like kissing your sister. I guess it's better than kissing your brother.

—LOU HOLTZ, after his Arkansas Razorbacks and UCLA tied in the 1978 Fiesta Bowl

Towns without Pity

BOSTON

Boston is the most prejudiced city in the United States of America.

> —BILL RUSSELL, who starred there 13
> seasons while leading the Celtics to 11
> NBA championships

CINCINNATI

The principal sport in Cincinnati is for people to sit on the front porch and watch the tar bubble in the street.

> —JIM MURRAY, columnist

CLEVELAND

The only difference between Cleveland and the Titanic is that the Titanic had better restaurants.

> —BARNEY NAGLER, sportswriter

The only good thing about playing in Cleveland is you don't have to make road trips there.

> —RICHIE SCHEINBLUM, Cleveland Indians
> outfielder

If you're going to have a plane crash in Cleveland, it's better to have one on the way in than on the way out.

> —PETER GAMMONS, baseball writer and
> commentator

HOUSTON

This is the only town where women wear insect repellant instead of perfume.

—RICHIE ALLEN, slugger turned sportscaster

NEW YORK

I could never play in New York. The first time I ever came into a game there, I got into the bullpen car and they told me to lock the doors.

—MIKE FLANAGAN, pitcher

If I was looking for Josef Mengele, my first thought would be to check the ushers in Yankee Stadium.

—BILL JAMES, author

Here is the beautiful thing about Fun City: It costs $4 to enter via the George Washington Bridge, but absolutely nothing to leave.

—GEORGE VECSEY, columnist

PHILADELPHIA

Philadelphia fans boo funerals, an Easter egg hunt, a parade of armless war vets and the Liberty Bell.

—BO BELINSKY, Phillies pitcher

SAN DIEGO

The good news is that we may stay in San Diego. The bad news, I guess, is the same thing.

> —BUZZIE BAVASI, Padres president, in an announcement about the team's future

SAN FRANCISCO

All the people of San Francisco want to do is go out to eat and go to the hookers ball.

> —REGGIE JACKSON, who knows the Bay Area from his seasons with the A's

WASHINGTON

Washington—first in war, first in peace, last in the American League.

> —CHARLES DRYDEN, writer, when the nation's capital had a baseball team

The Trading Post

We didn't want to weaken the rest of the league.

> —FRANK LANE, general manager, on why his Milwaukee Brewers hadn't made any trades

I always felt the more Browns I could place on other teams, the better off we would be.

> —BILL VEECK, owner of the hapless St. Louis Browns before the team moved to Baltimore and became the Orioles

You just bought yourself a cripple.

> —BILL TERRY, New York Giants player-manager, sneering at the New York Yankees for purchasing prospect Joe DiMaggio, who had a gimpy knee

What did we get for him? We got somebody who'll pay his salary.

> —TED TURNER, Atlanta Braves owner, after dumping lame-armed Andy Messersmith and his $300,000 salary on the New York Yankees, for whom he'd be 0–3 during his only season in pinstripes

This is the greatest thing that's happened to the Bears in five years. We got rid of those malcontents. It's a great day, a great day!

> —GEORGE "PAPA BEAR" HALAS, Chicago Bears owner, after trading away three players, including team player rep Mac Percival

You and your picket signs are going to New Orleans!

> —NORM VAN BROCKLIN, Atlanta Falcons coach, to player rep Ken Reaves during the 1974 NFL players' strike season

We played him and now we can't trade him.

> —BUZZIE BAVASI, Brooklyn Dodgers executive, on infielder Don Zimmer, a play-me-or-trade-me player

You've gone from Cy Young to Sayonara in one year.

> —GRAIG NETTLES, New York Yankees third base-
> man, to Sparky Lyle after the one-time award-winning
> southpaw was traded from the Bronx to Texas

Sometimes the best deals are the ones you don't make.

> —BILL VEECK, Hall of Famer, who constantly bartered
> during four memorable stints as a baseball owner

Umpires, Advice from

Boys, I'm one of those umpires that can make a mistake on the close ones. So if it's close, you'd better hit it.

> —CAL HUBBARD, umpire

Umpires, Advice to

Haven't you ever worn a mask before? You're supposed to look through the open spaces *between* the bars.

> —GEORGE "BIRDIE" TEBBETTS, catcher,
> to the plate umpire a moment before he
> was awarded the rest of the afternoon off

Umpires and Referees

Kill him! He hasn't any friends!

> —Familiar cry against umpires during baseball's early
> days—until the time of World War I, when it
> was condensed to a terse:

Kill the umpire!

>   —Familiar cry ever since

The average umpire is a worthless loafer.

>   —*Chicago Tribune*, 1880

Umpiring is best described as the profession of standing between two seven-year-olds with one ice cream cone.

>   —RON LUCIANO, umpire turned author

Many baseball fans look upon an umpire as a sort of necessary evil to the luxury of baseball, like the odor that follows an automobile.

>   —CHRISTY MATHEWSON, Hall of Fame pitcher

If the Pope was an umpire, he'd still have trouble with the Catholics.

>   —BEANS REARDON, umpire

I've been mobbed, cussed, booed, kicked in the ass, punched in the face, hit with mud balls and whisky bottles, and had everything from shoes to fruits and vegetables thrown at me.
  An umpire should hate humanity.

>   —JOE RUE, umpire

They shot the wrong McKinley.

>   —JIMMY PIERSALL, Boston Red Sox outfielder, to veteran umpire Bill McKinley, an instant before McKinley ejected him

In a way an umpire is like a woman. He makes quick decisions, never reverses them, and doesn't think you're safe when you're out.

> —LARRY GOETZ, umpire

I occasionally get birthday cards from fans. But it's often the same message: they hope it's my last.

> —AL FORMAN, umpire

When I'm right, no one remembers. When I'm wrong, no one forgets.

> —DOUG HARVEY, umpire

I never questioned the integrity of an umpire. Their eyesight, yes.

> —LEO DUROCHER, champion umpire baiter

How could he be doing his job when he didn't throw me out of the game after the things I called him?

> —MARK BELANGER, shortstop, on umpire Russ Goetz

Logic? Umpires? If they had any logic they wouldn't be doing this for a living.

> —DOUG RADER, manager

Umpiring's tough...you're always half wrong.

> —BILL WHITE, first baseman turned broadcaster turned National League president

What are you sore about? Your favorite team won, didn't it?

> —CASEY STENGEL, Boston Bees manager, to umpire Larry Goetz the day after the Brooklyn Dodgers clinched the 1941 pennant in Boston

Now, what the hell. Do you think I'd admit that?

> —AUGIE DONATELLI, umpire, on whether he'd ever missed a call

It [use of electronic umpires] will never happen, because when you do that you've taken away all the alibis.

Who can the managers blame losses on? Who can pitchers and hitters blame their troubles on?

Believe me, the umpire will always be with us.

> —BEANS REARDON, retired umpire

The ref brought his lunch.
The ref brought his lunch.
Eat it ref, eat it.

> —American football cheer, circa 1955

Umpiring Arrogance

It ain't anything 'til I call it.

> —BILL KLEM, Hall of Fame umpire

Anytime I got those "bang-bang" plays at first base, I called 'em out. It made the game shorter.

> —TOM GORMAN, umpire and author

They didn't get a very good look at you, did they?

> —JOCKO CONLON, veteran umpire, to Boston Braves
> catcher Del Crandall, whom he ejected after the
> game's second pitch despite the 19-year-old rookie's
> protestations that his parents had traveled across
> the country to see his Boston debut

Crandall would have had more opportunity to make a longer impression on his parents if only the brash teenager hadn't instructed the umpire to "Call 'em right, you [bleep]."

Maybe I called it wrong, but it's official.

> —TOMMY CONNOLLY, five-foot-seven umpiring giant,
> during his 1898–1931 career

If you don't think you're out, read the morning paper.

> —BILL McGOWAN, umpire, to a former
> baserunner

The Usual Suspects

The sports section needs a crime page.

> —MIKE LUPICA, columnist

If cocaine were helium, the whole NBA would float away.

> —ART RUST, sportscaster

If [convicted felon and Cy Young Award winner] Dennis McLain has a couple of bad outings for his prison team, will he be released?

> —MIKE LUPICA, columnist

If I wasn't in boxing, I'd be breaking the law. That's my nature.

> —MIKE TYSON, heavyweight champ, before his rape
> conviction

Violence

Sportsmanship and easygoing methods are all right, but it's the prospect of a hot fight that brings out the crowd.

> —JOHN McGRAW, New York Giants manager

We're going to have to do something about all this violence, or people are going to keep buying tickets.

> —CONN SMYTHE, Toronto Maple Leafs general manager

There has never been any violence in the NHL.

> —CLARENCE CAMPBELL, league president, commenting on a government-sponsored report that blamed the NHL for setting a bad example for Canadian youth

If you keep the opposition on their asses, they don't score goals.

> —FRED SHERO, coach of the Philadelphia Flyers' "Broad Street Bullies" in the seventies

I wouldn't set out to hurt anybody deliberately unless it was, you know, important—like a league game or something.

> —DICK BUTKUS, Chicago Bears linebacker

I never make a tackle just to bring someone down. I want to punish the man I'm going after and I want him to know that it's going to hurt every time he comes my way.

> —JACK TATUM, Oakland Raiders defensive back, whose 1978 tackle of Darryl Stingley rendered the New England Patriots receiver a quadriplegic

Is it normal to wake up in the morning in a sweat because you can't wait to beat another human's guts out?

> —JOE KAPP, quarterback

If I don't kill him it doesn't count.

> —MIKE TYSON, onetime heavyweight champion

I don't throw the first punch. I throw the second four.

> —BILLY MARTIN, baseball player and manager, who had plenty of experience

The only rule I had in fighting was to get in the first punch whenever possible. Basketball fights rarely go beyond two or three punches, and the player who scores first usually wins.

> —"JUNGLE JIM" LOSCUTOFF, Boston Celtics enforcer

Walking

I like long walks, especially when they're taken by people who annoy me.

> —FRED ALLEN, humorist

War (Real)

To hell with Babe Ruth!

> —Japanese battle cry during World War II.

War (Unreal)

People don't seem to understand that it's a damned war out there.... I don't go out there to love my enemy. I go out there to squash him.

      —JIMMY CONNORS, tennis pro

The War between the Sexes

Women as a group have a long way to go before they reach the level of intensity and dedication to sports that enables men to be such incredible jerks about it.

      —DAVE BARRY, columnist

Women can't play a lick. I'll prove that. I'll set women's tennis back 20 years.

      —BOBBY RIGGS, before his historic match against Billie Jean King in the Astrodome

Forty years ago women were playing tennis in floppy hats and funny dresses. Now Bobby Riggs is doing it.

      —BILLIE JEAN KING

The War between the Sexes II: Olson vs. Kiam

What a classic bitch! The players can't stand her.

      —VICTOR KIAM, New England Patriots owner, on *Boston Herald* sportswriter Lisa Olson, whose sexual harassment case against the Patriots was settled out of court

What do the Iraquis have in common with Lisa Olson? They've both seen the Patriot missiles up close.

> —VICTOR KIAM, addressing a Connecticut banquet

Gag that man with a jock strap.

> —ELLEN GOODMAN, *Boston Globe* columnist, on Victor Kiam

What Becomes a Legend Least

Mantle burped at the fans until he lived to be 50 and needed to become a grand old guy.

> —GEORGE VECSEY, columnist, on The Mick

He treats fans with contempt and sportswriters even worse.

> —MURRAY CHASS, sportswriter, on New York Yankees veteran Graig Nettles

I don't mind being called a prick or a cocksucker or things like that. I expect that. But lay off the personal stuff.

> —BABE RUTH, who knew where to draw the line

Some people are leaders and some are followers. I'm a follower.

> —MICKEY MANTLE, who led in a number of categories—while leading the New York Yankees to a string of championships

What Goes Up...

The hero of a thousand plays becomes a bum after one error.

> —BOB ZUPPKE, college football coach

To an athlete or coach, a thousand words of praise are negated by one word of criticism by the writer.

> —GEORGE SULLIVAN, sportswriter

When to Hire a Public Relations Firm

Who is this Baby Ruth and what does she do?

> —GEORGE BERNARD SHAW, during a visit to America

Wimbledon

Wimbledon is a reminder of what tennis was like before it died.

> —DAN JENKINS, novelist and humorist

Winning

I come to win.

—LEO DUROCHER

Once you start keeping score, winning's the bottom line. It's the American concept.

—AL McGUIRE, basketball player, coach, and broadcaster

I don't even let my 10-year-old daughter beat me at Tic-Tac-Toe.

—BOB GIBSON, Hall of Fame pitcher

Winning isn't everything; it's the only thing.

—VINCE LOMBARDI

Win any way you can, as long as you can get away with it.

—LEO DUROCHER

There are only two places in the league: first place and no place.

—TOM SEAVER, Hall of Fame pitcher

Root only for the winner. That way you won't be disappointed.

—TUG McGRAW, pitcher

If you can accept losing, you can't win.

> —VINCE LOMBARDI

What are we out at the park for except to win? I'd trip my mother. I'd help her up, brush her off, tell her I'm sorry. But mother doesn't make it to third base.

> —LEO DUROCHER

I've got to be first. All the time.

> —TY COBB, who once fought his roommate over first use of their hotel bathroom

Winning and Losing

I'd rather be a poor winner than any kind of loser.

> —GEORGE S. KAUFMAN, playwright

The joy of winning doesn't motivate me anymore. It's the fear of losing.

> —RANDY MATSON, world champion shot-putter

Every time you win, you're reborn. When you lose, you die a little.

> —GEORGE ALLEN, NFL coach

In that case, why keep score?

> —DONALD DELL, tennis agent and commentator, reacting to those who suggest winning or losing isn't important—only "how you play the game"

Winning Attitudes

I have no intention or desire to win 20 games, because they keep expecting it of you.

—BILLY LOES, Brooklyn Dodgers pitcher

Winter Olympics

Part of the charm of the Winter Olympics is that ice skating and all the rest of those Olympic sports completely disappear for four years at a time.

—DAN JENKINS, novelist and humorist

Women in the Locker Room

Madam, I see where you don't seem to mind male nudity in the athletes' shower room at sports arenas. Well, neither would any whore.

—Beginning of a letter, signed "Male Senior,"
to Alison Gordon after her first season
covering the Blue Jays for the *Toronto Star*

Gordon framed the letter and hung it in her bathroom.

All she's got to do is learn how to do two things: Stand up at the bar and buy a round of drinks and stand up at the urinal and piss.

—EARLY WYNN, pitcher turned broadcaster, joking
on what it would take for Alison Gordon to become a
sportswriter

If they want to take their clothes off and talk to the players, fine. But I warn them—they'll have a lot more trouble getting out than they did getting in.

>—HAROLD BALLARD, Toronto Maple Leafs owner

It's an invasion of privacy. It's indecent. You might as well interview me while I'm sitting on the pot.

>—ROY FOSTER, Miami Dolphins guard

I don't care. I treat every reporter the same. Like crap.

>—MIKE BAAB, Cleveland Browns center, on women reporters vs. men reporters

Watch out, here comes the pecker checker!

>—A Detroit Tiger's shout as Toronto sportswriter Alison Gordon entered his team's locker room

Earl Weaver, Baltimore Orioles manager, disputed that description of Gordon, whom he liked. Weaver introduced the sportswriter to his wife, saying, "Marianne, this is Alison. She ain't no pecker checker. She's okay."

"You can tell the *New York Times* to kiss my dago ass."

>—Billy Martin to reporter Deborah Henschel after the New York Yankees manager ordered the researcher to halt her survey in the Yankees locker room and "get your ass out of my clubhouse," to which Henschel reacted, "But I'm from the *New York Times*"

The incident ignited a lingering brouhaha that included a formal protest by the Times, *which also charged that Martin had called Henschel a "slut" and a "hussy."*

At the very least, Martin impugned the woman's fashion sense, telling Yankee investigators that Henschel didn't look like a working reporter, claiming she was "wearing a low-cut dress with slits up to here."

Won't You Be My Neighbor?

Most people can't afford to live where I live. That's why I live there.

—REGGIE JACKSON, in a world of his own

Words from the Husbands

Yes, I did.

—JOE DiMAGGIO, to Marilyn Monroe
on their Japan honeymoon,
after the bride returned from a
sidetrip to entertain U.S.
troops in Korea and reported to
her husband, "Joe, Joe. You
never heard such cheering"

Don't come unless you know how to set a broken leg.

—CASEY STENGEL, in a Boston hospital with a fractured fibula and tibia, to his wife, Edna, at home in
California attending her ill mother

Words from the Wives

My turn at bat was no ball.

> —DELORES WILLIAMS, former wife of
> Ted Williams (author of *My Turn at
> Bat*), speculating on the title of *her* auto-
> biography

Ball Who? and *Breaking Balls*.

> —Titles considered but rejected for the book *Home
> Games,* co-authored by former baseball wives
> Bobbie Bouton and Nancy Marshall

It was too bad I wasn't a second baseman; then I'd probably have seen a lot more of my husband.

> —KAROLYN ROSE, first wife of Pete Rose

What does a first-base coach do besides pat guys on the rear end?

> —CAROLE MERRILL, upon hearing her husband,
> Stump, had been named the New York Yankees
> first base coach

Stump allegedly replied: "Nothing. How about some practice?"

For the rest of his career he [husband/pitcher Bob Stanley] is going to take the blame for this. And he shouldn't. I mean, I love Geddy [catcher Rich Gedman], I really do, but he blew it, you know. He blew it.

> —JOAN STANLEY, shifting the blame from her spouse to his batterymate for the infamous wild pitch that allowed the Mets to tie the Red Sox in the 10th inning of game six in the 1986 World Series—moments before a weak grounder trickled between Boston first baseman Bill Buckner's legs for New York's mind-blowing victory

He's more likely to die on a 16-foot yacht with a 60-year-old mistress.

> —BETSY CRONKITE, whose sailor/anchorman husband Walter had been quoted as saying he'd like to die on a 60-foot yacht in the company of a 16-year-old mistress

I'm much more sexual than my husband. I need a man more than he needs a woman.

> —CYNDY GARVEY, on her former husband, Steve

You are a foul ball in the line drive of life.

> —LUCY, to Charlie Brown

World's Worst Predictions

The baseball mania has run its course. It has no future as a professional endeavor.

> —*Cincinnati Gazette*, 1879

I'll moider da bum!

> —"TWO-TON" TONY GALENTO, a New Jersey
> saloon keeper and boxer, predicting opponent Joe
> Louis' fate in their 1939 heavyweight title match
> at Yankee Stadium

Galento managed to floor Louis in the third round before the champion knocked out the challenger a round later.

I find soccer an exciting sport, with long-range potential as a television attraction.

> —BARRY FRANK, CBS Sports vice president, after
> the network signed a three-year contract with the
> North American Soccer League

Winning is the epitome of honesty itself.

> —WOODY HAYES, football coach, in September 1977,
> the day before his Ohio State Buckeyes were beaten
> on a 41-yard field goal with three seconds left, 29–28

The Giants is dead.

> —CHARLIE DRESSEN, Brooklyn Dodgers manager,
> before the archrival New York Giants caught fire and
> made up a 13½-game deficit, overtaking the Dodgers
> on Bobby Thomson's play-off home run for the 1951
> pennant

Zipping into Oblivion

I thinks, me lads, this is me last slide.

> —MICHAEL "KING" KELLY, early baseball
> hero and Hall of Famer, on his Boston
> deathbed at age 46 in 1894

GEORGE SULLIVAN has spent a lifetime in professional sports beginning at age fifteen when he made his debut as a Boston Red Sox batboy. A former Boston sportswriter/columnist and the author of six books, Sullivan has also served as Public Relations Director for the Red Sox and Vice President of Communications at Suffolk Downs. He credits his lifetime in sports for turning him into the curmudgeon that he is today.

BARBARA LAGOWSKI is a former book editor and the author of eleven books, including fiction, nonfiction, and humor. She is planning to file for disability on the basis of her longtime allegiance to the Boston Red Sox.